Emotional Intelligence For Leadership

How to Hack Your Brain, Uncover Your Full Potential and Become a Leader that Influences, Inspires and Empowers People and Your Team to Take Action for a better life

Deniel Clark & David Goleman

TABLE OF CONTENTS

Introduction

Effective communication is a very important skill which you must learn if you want to move ahead in your career. No matter what you do and what your intentions are but if you cannot communicate effectively then, your whole idea of progressing will fail.

You cannot tell your plans and goals without an effective communication technique. If you are confused while explaining something then, people will think that will also be confused while attempting that thing. This is natural gesture which every normal person will give you.

You would have seen around that there are some people with a very confident and alert tone and these people always tend to be more successful and managed in their lives than those who lack self-confidence and effective communication skills.

This is not because the second types of people do not have the working capabilities but it is just that they cannot motivate people to work for them and they can never convince people effectively to team up with them.

There are certain techniques which can help you out in enhancing your effective communication skills and these techniques will tell you exactly what you lack in being a good speaker as well as a very good listener. Some people think that just speaking and expressing is communication but you should know that listening is another very important part of the communication. When you listen then, you can express yourself and these expressions encourage or discourage the speaker to continue his talks.

Acquiring and keeping a good workforce or strong staff base is very important to any business endeavor whether it is small or big. Therefore in the quest to keep all parties happy and functioning the key is to practice good communication always. Good communication allows the smooth flow of information to be divulged and accepted by all parties thus creating a clear picture of what is expected and desired.

Without communication there is the real possibility of encountering problems simply because everyone is doing what they think is best thus not coordinating and working as a team. The results of this are usually unpleasant and definitely not positive.

Good communication skill will also help to establish the individual in the business arena, thus creating the platform for respect and authority in the particular venture. This will also help to ensure customers will be more than willing to generate return sales due to the effective communication expounded. Communication does not only mean divulging information, it also means having a keen listening ear. This is a highly prized element for customers and is definitely well received, when the tone of the communication clearly shows the business owner understands the customers' needs.

Good communication also ensures fewer mistakes are made and this is also another important fact to be conscious of. Not considering its importance, could eventually lead to costly mistakes, some of which are not easy to recover from.

Communication is an essential process which helps us to express our feelings and without communication, we will not be able to share our knowledge and experiences with other people.

There are different parts of communication like speaking, listening, gestures, and body language while each one of these is important to make communication effective. When you can master these all parts then, you can say that you have learned the art of effective communication.

Communication skills have a very deep importance in any business environment and effective or ineffective communication can make organizations progressive or declined respectively. You can never say that communication has become ideal in some organization just because some of the language glitches are fixed instead communication is a thing which always needs your attention and constant maintenance and improvement. While communicating at interpersonal level, you should make sure that the meaning of your discussion is properly understood by the listener. Just saying "do you know what I mean" in the end will not be sufficient.

You can always make a map that which damages and advantages you can get from ineffective and effective communication. This will not take that long to know that ineffective communication can give you lots of losses in terms of your work, time, productivity, progress and other similar things.

If you have mis-communicated with your boss over a certain report then, you will have to do that report from scratch and it will cost you both time and work and in most of the cases ineffective communication will cause you embarrassment. The best approach is to identify miscommunication as soon as possible because sooner you identify sooner you can fix it.

Ineffective communication will also cause you lots of extra stress and tension because when you miss some work due to ineffective communication then, your boss will be angry with you and it may happen that some of your colleague also gets disturbed with that effort. So it can disturb the whole working environment for you. In order to avoid all of the above problems, you must communicate effectively and if you are having problems in effective communication then, you must keep reading, improving your communication and your leadership as well.

Reasons Why Emotional Intelligence is Vital for Leaders

Emotional intelligence is defined by the ability to understand and manage your emotions and the emotions of those around you. This particular quality provides you with a variety of skills like the ability to maintain relationships, influence and inspire others, and how to navigate social networks. To become an effective leader, you need to have a high level of emotional intelligence. Here are some of the most essential reasons why emotional information is vital for leaders.

Self-Awareness

Great and useful leaders that have high emotional intelligence are that they are self-aware, and they can recognize emotions as they happen. This is an incredibly vital skill if you want to be a great leader because it can help you obtain a clear understanding of your particular strengths and weaknesses. When you have self-awareness, you are better able to perceive emotions as they arise in response to an action or situation.

Emotional Management

Having high emotional intelligence means that you are able to manage your emotions and stay in control effectively. When you can manage your feelings, you are unlikely to rush headlong into decisions or let anger take over your behavior. To be an effective leader, you have to be able to keep your emotions in check.

Effective Communication

If you aren't effective at communicating, you'll be unable to clearly express your thoughts, which is an essential aspect of leadership. When you have high emotional intelligence, you can clearly convey directions and know what needs to be said to inspire and motivate your employees. Communication is an essential skill that all leaders need to have because it can be the deciding factor in whether or not your team listens.

Social Awareness

Leaders that have high levels of emotional intelligence are well tuned into the emotions of others and are able to pick up on what is happening around them effectively. They can sympathize with others and providing helpful feedback. Leaders who are looking to inspire and motivate their employees having social awareness is a critical skill. If, as a leader, you are unable to empathize with your employees, you will find it challenging to obtain the respect and loyalty of your employees.

Conflict Resolution

In every workplace, there is always the risk that conflicts will disrupt the efficiency and productivity of the office. With high emotional intelligence, you are better equipped to handle disputes and provide resolutions to conflicts. With this skill, you can quickly satisfy any disagreements that might arise between your employees.

Self-Regulation

Self-regulation, or discipline, involves your ability to control or redirect your disruptive emotions and being able to adapt to changing circumstances to keep your team moving in the right direction. Being calm is contagious. As a leader, you can't afford to panic when things get a bit too stressful. When you can learn to stay calm and positive, you are better able to think and communicate more clearly.

Empathy and Compassion

Empathy is your ability to put yourself in someone else's shoes so you can understand how they feel and react appropriately to the situation. When you have empathy, your capacity to feel compassion is higher. The emotions that you feel in response to suffering is what motivates a desire in you to help. The more you can relate to those around you, the better you'll come to understand what motivates and upsets them.

Relationship Management

If you're distracted, you will never be able to make deep connections with others. Everyone has family obligations and a crazy to-do list, but being able to build and maintain healthy relationships is essential to your ability to boost your emotional intelligence, You have to have the ability to communicate effectively and maintain relationships if you want to move people in the right direction within your organization.

Effective Communication

Effective communication is of the utmost importance when it comes to being an effective leader. Recent studies have shown that communication is seven percent the words you say and 93 percent tone and body language. Misunderstandings and lack of communication are usually the basis of problems between people. Failing to communicate effectively at work leads to frustration, confusion, and bitterness among employees. When you are competent at communicating, you can eliminate obstacles and encourage stronger relationships within your company.

If you want to become a more effective leader, then you have to work on improving your emotional intelligence. With a higher emotional intelligence, you can become a more effective leader and develop a more productive work environment.

Your main job as a leader is to be a guiding light to others, inspiring people with your 'voice of leadership', transforming their lack of clarity and confidence into hopefulness and resolve in moving forward.

Successful leaders and managers today are willing to exercise their leadership in such a way that their people are empowered to make decisions, share information, and try new things. Most employees (future leaders) see the value in finding empowerment and are willing to take on the responsibilities that come with it. If future leaders have the wisdom to learn from the experience of present leaders, and if present leaders have the wisdom to build an environment that empowers people, both will share in the benefits.

Motivational problems can lead to performance issues that cost a business thousands of dollars in losses each year. A lack of motivation can lead to delays in the employee's completion of work and simple but expensive mistakes. By supporting and encouraging involvement, you are helping employees create a sense of connection that extends across departmental boundaries

Chapter 1

DARK PSYCHOLOGY AND HUMAN MIND

Dark Psychology is the craftsmanship and study of manipulation and brain manipulation. While Psychology is the investigation of human conduct and is fundamental to our musings, activities, and co-operations, the term Dark Psychology is the wonder by which individuals use strategies of inspiration, influence, manipulation, and compulsion to get what they need.

In dark brain science, manipulation lies at the core of the incredible secret that is human insight and cognizance. There are numerous stunts and techniques to be learned and used, which release the potential outcomes you never imagined existed. We, as people, become skilled at introducing to the world a façade that can be split and manipulated utilizing demonstrated and investigated strategies, which you would now be able to find yourself through training. Neuro-semantic programming offers an entirely different procedure to take a gander at correspondence and the various methods for passing on data. You currently realize what to look like for unobtrusive signs like small scale articulations to distinguish how somebody is feeling about you, which gives you an update regarding how you're accomplishing while you work to execute and complete your arrangements for someone else.

One of the fundamental devices right now figuring out how to recognize when somebody is attempting to utilize vile strategies on you, the more you instruct yourself on the standards and methodologies of dark brain research, the more you figure out how to remember them at whatever point they are being utilized and in whatever setting you end up in. As you are currently furnished with this data, it is more uncertain for you to get yourself a casualty of somebody talented in expressions of the human experience of dark brain science. You can distinguish the narcissist or sociopath in the room, maybe after even only a couple of discussions with the people.

There are a wide range of character types on the planet, and you presently have a superior comprehension of what those different character parts, how they cooperate, and how you can recognize them through direct connections and examination. You see how chilly understanding functions and you are definitely not guileless with regards to individuals attempting to persuade you that they find out about you then you might suspect. You will have the option to get on this promptly and have figured out how individuals plant the seeds in others' psyches to persuade them that they have information well beyond what they really have.

Over the most recent couple of years, the "Positive Psychology" development has been extremely popular. We should quit fussing about the underside of human instinct and study individuals who are cheerful, bold, profitable, and self-completed!

Be that as it may, Del Paulhus has resisted the pattern with a progression of studies digging into the clouded side of human character. As he notes in a paper discharged today in Current Directions in Psychological Science: "Our work on the 'clouded side' remains as a distinct difference to the well-known work on constructive character attributes, in our view, dark characters are more entrancing than sparkling, upbeat people."

Paulhus and his partners have identified four various types of conceited and socially hostile individuals who the vast majority of us experience in our everyday lives: narcissists, Machiavellians, nonclinical sociopaths, and regular cruel people.

Paulhus noticed that therapists regularly befuddle these sorts of people, who all offer an inclination to score particularly high on proportions of insensitivity (or absence of compassion for others). Every one of these sorts likewise will, in general, be outgoing and amiable, so frequently establish great first connections, before proceeding to make life hopeless for the individuals who are misused by them. In any case, there are significant contrasts, and those differentiations have significant ramifications for the sorts of mischief these people can do to their relationship accomplices and associates.

Narcissists are "vainglorious self-advertisers who consistently long for consideration." Paulhus takes note of that: "You have without a doubt been irritated by these tedious showoffs." Frank Sinatra, the extraordinary crooner of my mom's age, was something of a narcissist, a quality he imparted to any number of hotshots in the performing expressions, at that point and now.

Machiavellians, as per Paulhus, are "Ace manipulators... one of them has bamboozled you out of something important—a reality that you might not have acknowledged until it was past the point of no return." They contrast from narcissists in their particularly high scores on a trial of manipulative, and their tendency to be associated with professional wrongdoing. The stock swindler Bernard Madoff, who stirred his way up to the authority of the New York Stock Exchange, just to utilize his situation to bilk his financial specialists out of a huge number of dollars, is the exemplary Macchiavellian.

Insane people, as Paulhus notes, are "apparently the most malignant," scoring high on proportions of insensitivity, impulsivity, manipulative, and self-importance, accordingly being dark in all cases. They regularly damage to others as they approach looking for thrills with little worry for who gets injured en route. Their indiscretion makes them less capable of cubicle wrongdoing of the Bernie Madoff assortment and regularly slants them towards brutality when others hinder them. Charles Manson and Whitey Bulger are great instances of psychopathy (see Do You Have Criminal Genes?). Yet, Paulhus noticed that there are numerous individuals whose psychopathy is sufficiently low to shield from arriving in prison, while all things considered prompting costs for the individuals who are gravitated toward to them.

What is particularly alarming about this initially set (the first "Dark Triad") is that they are regularly socially proficient, and can establish generally excellent first connections. For instance, they improve on prospective employee meetings than ordinary individuals, advantaged by their absence of nervousness about the assessments of others, and more prominent readiness to flaunt their qualities to outsiders while playing it smooth and agreeable.

Ordinary twisted people share the attribute of hardness with the initial three sorts, however, they are recognized not by their lack of caution or manipulative (which are in the typical range), yet rather by their pleasure in brutality. As Paulhus notes, regular twisted people might be attracted to employments, for example, cops or the military, where they can hurt others in a genuine pretense. Paulhus isn't stating, by chance, that all law implementation faculty are vicious, however basically that their positions may have a higher than normal number of regular savages (who, as confirmed by a police officer met as of late on NPR, can harm police-network relations).

On the off chance that you read Paulhus' paper, you may begin to ponder about its writer - for what reason would anybody be attracted to investigate on narcissism, psychopathy, and perversion? I have known Paulhus for at any rate two decades and delighted in numerous discussions with him during long strolls around Vancouver (generally after dark, in light of the fact that he is a night owl). He is definitely not a narcissist or a mental case, it turns out. Undoubtedly, he is an extremely decent person, humble, and a gathering player. When he read this blog entry at the beginning of today, he sent me this note: "Don't have the foggiest idea whether it destroys the stream, yet might you be able to stick in something about my few ages of understudy associates? In the event that there's space for their names, they are Kevin Williams,

Craig Nathanson, Peter Harms, Dan Jones, Erin Buckels." That's decidedly non-narcissistic!

Rather, Del is a modest piece thoughtful and exceptionally reliable, spending an extraordinary piece of his life working into the extremely early times while the remainder of his partners is sleeping soundly. What drives Del is an interest in the careful estimation of character attributes. Despite the fact that his work on the clouded side of the character is very notable, he is better known for his work uncovering reaction inclinations in character tests and recognizing the various types of social allure that can pollute our responses to those tests. He particularly wants to reveal differentiations that different analysts have missed, as in the qualification between self-trickiness versus impression the executives - that may lead two distinct individuals to rank themselves at the 90th percentile on "superbness" for various reasons (I am tricking myself, yet you may basically be attempting to trick potential businesses).

Paulhus' work on the clouded side of character comes from that equivalent logical module in his psyche. In the ongoing article on the clouded side of a character, he takes note of that he got into this region as a result of his anxiety about "build creep." He got stressed over how specialists who examined narcissism, for instance, without all the while pondering Machiavellianism or psychopathy, would begin to grow the term to envelop the other related, however unmistakable, ideas. Paulhus thinks it is basically essential to recognize the various sorts of dark characters, on the grounds that there are commonsense outcomes - a worker who is Machiavellian will do an alternate sort of harm than one who is narcissistic or psychopathic, for instance. Since these people share an inclination to do well in beginning connections, Paulhus contends that it is significant that businesses utilize great clean proportions of those builds as a major aspect of their workforce appraisal batteries. What's more, in light of what a portion of my companions have let me know, a few people would have gotten a kick out of the chance to have those estimations close by before they picked their long haul mates.

Chapter 2

THE ETHICS OF COMMUNICATION

It is ordinary nowadays to catch wind of an organization's code of ethical, yet ethical correspondence is regularly not tended to in the conversation, despite the fact that it is a basic component of the organization's prosperity. Correspondence is fundamental in any relationship, however particularly when your business depends on its authority to convey clear and steady data to the workforce. Individuals rapidly gain proficiency with the contrast among communicated and genuine qualities, and instinctually know when an association is showcasing its qualities consistently and remunerating individuals that go the additional mile. Ethical correspondence ought to be a top-of-mind need for organization pioneers while tending to all partners – regardless of whether they are peers, staff, clients or financial specialists.

What Is Ethical Correspondence?

Ethical correspondence is essential to keen dynamic and capable reasoning. It is tied in with creating and supporting connections and building networks inside and across settings, societies, channels, and media. Ethical correspondence is additionally tolerating obligation regarding the messages you pass on to other people and the present moment or long haul outcomes of your correspondence. Regardless of whether you are conversing with a dear companion or tending to the workforce in an all-staff meeting, your message must be honest and predictable with your worth framework. Deluding your audience members and conveying a message that is furtive or not honest is the direct opposite of ethical correspondence.

Moreover, ethical correspondence may reach out to the medium or even the language you decide for conveying your message. Utilizing a medium that restricts the crowd or conveying a message in a language that your crowd doesn't completely comprehend, confines how your message is gotten and seen. For instance, on the off chance that you are addressing a crowd of people of essentially hard of hearing or hearing-impeded representatives, ethical correspondence requires having correspondence via gestures mediator.

At the point when you are not imparting ethically, audience members wonder if what you are stating is valid. Absence of ethical correspondence drives others to scrutinize your expert and individual honesty and to think about whether they can confide in your message, or even trust you. When you have lost individuals' regard and trust, you should work twice as difficult to get it back, and at times you can't, regardless of how hard you attempt. For instance, an organization president who guarantees laborers that the organization will remain family-claimed declares a half year later that a huge aggregate has purchased the business. She will lose the trust of her workers, and they will question anything she says in the future.

Notwithstanding, a Hill+Knowlton Strategies review on supportability, straightforwardness and business execution, uncovered that 82 percent of the 1,000 respondents accepted that an organization could recover trust on the off chance that it was responsible and gave a fair and straightforward report on how it was attempting to be increasingly economical. Turns out people in general and workers needn't bother with an organization to be great, they simply need straightforwardness and honesty more than anything. Through the procedure of ethical correspondence, you ought to concede you missed the mark regarding your objectives, which at last prepares for immense upgrades in the future and backing from every one of your partners.

Standards of Ethical Correspondence

Ethical correspondence has a few standards or central components. Imparting reality-based messages genuinely and precisely is key to ethical correspondence. Ethical correspondence esteems opportunity of articulation, assorted variety of points of view and resilience of difference. Be that as it may, while ethical correspondence ought to be straightforward and clear, it ought to never affront or incite audience members.

Ethical correspondence permits access to the assets and realities that planned the message. For instance, on the off chance that you are sharing data about stock execution, you are committed to giving your crowd yearly reports, filings with the Securities and Exchange Commission or investor reports.

Conveying in an ethical way additionally requires making the message open. This implies in the event that you are conveying a message to a huge or assorted crowd, guarantee that you oblige the dialects and listening inclinations of everyone. Despite the fact that the official language in the U.S. is English, there are a large number of guests and lawful occupants whose first language isn't English. To convey a message that can be comprehended by a different crowd requires connecting with language specialists or interpreters who can help you in making the message open to all.

Notwithstanding making the message available and regarding the decent variety of thought and viewpoint, ethical correspondence implies being a kind of essential human needs. Maintaining a strategic distance from words and language that are disparaging or narrow-minded and shunning messages that advance or prompt savagery is central to ethical correspondence.

Ethical Correspondence in the Workplace

Correspondence in the working environment happens at all levels; director to worker, administrator to boss and officials to representatives – one-on-one and in bunch settings. For instance, a manager conveying a presentation survey to a representative ought to keep ethical correspondence measures.

While tending to a high-performing worker, a chief must find some kind of harmony by adulating extraordinary execution in certain territories with thoughts for development in others. On the other hand, an audit of a worker who is performing at an average level should be real to life with the goal that the representative can see their activity shortcomings from the administrator's point of view, which permits her to concentrate on improving in those zones. A chief must impart sincerely and honestly to her representatives by giving acknowledgment for solid execution and instructing or direction now and again when the worker needs to refocus and meet the organization's desires.

Backing for the organization's vision streams down from official initiative to staff, the messages that top heads in the organization convey to center administration, line chiefs and staff must be straightforward. Perhaps the least demanding approach to pick up the certainty of your representatives is being straightforward and clear with them in the entirety of your interchanges. At the point when pioneers are honest, they procure the help of staff and directors.

Instances of Ethical Communication

Ever wonder why news sources have reality checkers, particularly during effort season? During the last days of a battle season, government officials have been known to either exaggerate or not advise every bit of relevant information to pick up help from constituents and benefactors. Making effort guarantees that are difficult to keep is unscrupulous correspondence. A few lawmakers battle with accommodating ethical correspondence with powerful correspondence. In his 2014 article, "Ethical Dilemmas in the Use of Big Data Analytics (BDA) in Affecting Political Correspondence and Behavior," Kenneth Hacker investigates the utilization of huge information examination inside the setting of political crusade discourses. Large information examination or BDA is data that is valuable to support associations, and frequently people also, settle on choices dependent on relationships, examples, patterns, and inclinations.

For instance, say a legislator is attempting to collect help in a territory that once flourished with the distant memory steel industry. She tells the group she relates to their financial battle since the demise of the business that left the network without living-wage employments and accuses outside combinations who have usurped U.S. strength in the steel business. The government official is going after the vulnerabilities of the audience members by utilizing BDA to discover what evokes an emotional response from supporters – the pattern of a declining steel industry around there of the U.S., and the inclinations that voters would admission better with occupations that empower them to continue their previous way of life. This type of political influence isn't ethical correspondence since it isn't straightforward or direct, and it doesn't mirror reality with regards to the U.S. steel industry.

Step by step instructions to Teach Ethical Correspondence

To participate in ethical correspondence, you should grasp essential expert and individual ethical. To start with, your duty to coming clean is basic. The American Management Association describes ethical correspondence as "Truth is Job 1," since truth is the most basic part of the ethical correspondence. No organization needs to remember the Enron calamity where representatives were tricked by pioneers who didn't uncover their benefits would be useless.

Ethical correspondence may possibly be shown when the organization's initiative comprehends the effect of the message. For instance, on the off chance that you are addressing the transportation office about looming cutbacks, you ought to expect that delivery office workers will impart that data to the business division. The business division is subject to transportation to guarantee their requests are conveyed on schedule. The message you provide for the transportation division workers should be comprehensive and ought to consider the effect it will have on offices that rely upon its delivery administrations.

Encouraging ethical correspondence is tied in with showing ethicals and expert and ethical obligation – not exactly how to address representatives or partners. The substance of the message is essentially significant, similar to the conveyance of the message. With such a significant number of various methods of correspondence, it's fundamental to recognize what sort of data is OK to send electronically versus data that ought to be conveyed eye to eye. Obviously, execution surveys and representative disciplinary audits ought to be conveyed in a vis-à-vis meeting in light of the fact that the topic warrants it. Plus, most representatives value getting constructive input and helpful analysis face to face. Then again, it's satisfactory to send the declaration of a day away from work in the wake of Thanksgiving by means of email to all staff.

Understanding your crowd is a basic point in conveying ethical correspondence. Without a piece of decent information on the crowd, the delivery person can unconsciously irritate audience members or even convey a message that wasn't proposed for that crowd. In the event that the flag-bearer is a top organization official, she may require Cliffs Notes from the HR division to direct her on how best to convey data that is relied upon to maybe be inadequately gotten.

HR Role in Ethical Correspondence

The HR division ordinarily is the go-to office for worker correspondence. HR ought to be engaged with all messages to representatives, particularly those that originate from the most significant level of administration. Paul Gennaro, senior VP of corporate interchanges and boss correspondence official for AECOM, in a meeting with SHRM Online says, "It must be from the HR side – what are the estimations of the association? How would we measure execution? It is safe to say that we are strengthening ethical and respectability? Are we making it part of our way of life?" For instance, direction from HR administration in ethical correspondence can help the organization president to convey a message that is generally welcomed, consequently, Cliffs Notes from HR.

The HR division is commonly liable for creating messages that the administration will convey to representatives. HR additionally reacts to representatives' inquiries regarding the message. For instance, an HR staff part may draft an organization president's discourse and give her inquiries that representatives are probably going to pose. Notwithstanding composing the discourse, HR can likewise give answers to foreseen questions, or possibly advise the president how to guide representatives to the correct hotspot for a progressively complete answer. Notwithstanding setting up the substance of the message and Q&A, HR can set up the president for the conveyance of the discourse, as in the planning, what she should think about the crowd, for instance, a little gathering or an all-hands meeting, and give her tips on the most proficient method to not get guarded or disapprove of worker questions, instructing right now additionally incorporate guidance for breaking down the non-verbal correspondence of the crowd individuals to decide their reaction to her message.

Human character/behavior

Behavior, character and character are unmistakable levels in the advancement of the individual. At the point when individuals show pleasant behavior, we state they are adequate. At the following level, when they have character, they can achieve something. At a further level, being invested with 'character', they can make something unique.

Let us initially analyze behavior. Behavior is shallow and comes through preparing. It is a channel through which a man communicates. The energies for behavior originate from the essential feelings, while the energies for character originate from the psyche. The fundamental energies are brief reactions to a circumstance. The customary man who is famous for everybody carries on well, has affable habits and doesn't condemn anybody. He is entirely adequate in the public arena. In any case, if this is the place his development has halted, he can't achieve anything in the normal feeling of the word. He can't find a foundation or make an imprint in his calling. One dare not give up an intensity of lawyer to him or endow him with any resources for safety's sake while one voyage. In an issue of something including a material responsibility, he won't be solid. Behavior can be acceptable and respectable, however past that behavior doesn't go. Insignificant behavior, a simple instruction, and unimportant age or experience won't achieve something all alone.

The fundamental driving forces are fleeting. They comprehend what they see. They can be prepared and this preparation is utilized in circumstances where there is no weight on the individual. The propensities which are shaped in the indispensable become its behavior. All propensities that are gotten in the essential and composed at that level are just at the degree of behavior, on the grounds that the indispensable has no bearing. It can't recall how it acted three days prior. On the off chance that it should be amiable following after some admirable people, it tends to be in this way, however, the behavior is fleeting. On the off chance that somebody acts like a companion today, he might be a foe tomorrow.

At the point when an individual has created character, he can achieve something without anyone else.

Character is sorted out in the psyche. It has a memory and always remembers. At the point when the embodiment of the essential experience in which his behavior is gotten in the brain and sorted out well with the goal that the psyche acknowledges that as its focal bearing, at that point it becomes a character.

A man with character fits into that degree of society to which his character has risen. On the off chance that he has an honorable character or a profound character, he might be a humanitarian or a CEO. In the event that he has a character however his temperament is little, he can sort out and raise a family effectively. An individual with character can build up his own business, raise a family, and achieve a significant work in the general public. These are everything that numerous individuals have done. There are as of now a thousand organizations; one more will be set up. An individual with character can achieve and do what has just been done previously.

At the point when the brain becomes an integral factor, it by and large follows up on a feeling or puts together itself with respect to thought. It attempts to comprehend and starts to think and sort out itself. The indispensable doesn't think, it reacts to the circumstance, however the psyche tunes in to thought. Based on this thought, the psyche arranges its qualities. The brain gives its approval to specific practices which it has acknowledged as right. This behavior at that point turns into an example. The substance of that example depends on decency, on social qualities. The psychological comprehension depends on the possibility that what is significant must be regarded. When the brain acknowledges this, each behavior will be coordinated by that trademark. In the event that a mother instructors her youngster to be amenable to his granddad, the kid doesn't have any acquaintance with it ought to likewise be courteous to his uncle. In the event that the youngster's psyche, which is equipped for comprehension, gets the embodiment of this example of graciousness towards senior family members, the example gets ceaseless and his brain acknowledges it as a general course. Kids ought to be pleasant to their old family members. This one thought turns into a guide for the entirety of his behavior, which becomes a character. That is called self-bearing. As it were, the behavior of the youngster, the passionate driving forces, are guided by the psychological understanding which has acknowledged the estimation of pleasant behavior towards senior family members.

An individual with negligible behavior can adhere to guidelines, however, he can't think all alone, though character originates from the psyche and empowers the individual to complete an errand with self-bearing. Without mind coming into the image, character can't be framed. The focal point of character is mind, while the focal point of behavior is the transient fundamental feelings. Character has more noteworthy vitality than behavior since it is sponsored by thought and issues from an increasingly focal piece of the being. Behavior shows itself in a brief individual circumstance, while character shows itself in all circumstances which the general public has acknowledged and developed. Character manages each behavior. On the off chance that a man with character is eager, his aspiration will appear in all that he does.

What is character? Character is important to accomplish something in the public arena, however when something must be made over again, the character is required. Where character may dither to endeavor something totally new, character won't.

Character can achieve something unique, whatever the field is.

Character is more profound than character. It doesn't limit itself to a sorted out articulation as a character does. Character needs the help of the social and mental milieu. Since the mind is a thin living being which works on thought, it draws its qualities from the general degree of thought in the general public. Something in the individual has a sense of security in that atmosphere and afterward, the brain comprehends, the heart can be enthused about that comprehension and the body can work. Typically when psyche needs to consider something unique, it starts to shake. Character can't be focused on the brain. It couldn't care less whether any other person has endeavored a specific work previously. It has the activity to begin a crisp work in another field.

Character doesn't require the incidental help of social approval. After it has comprehended and the brain has assented, it has the creative mind to give a psychological feeling to that assent. When the psyche can picture something in its own creative mind, the heart doesn't stop for a second to discharge its eagerness for the achievement of the work. The help for the work originates from the Being which is over the psyche. On the off chance that the psyche is clear and the Being bolsters, it needn't bother with the help of the general public. That is the distinction between character and character. Character is an effective mental creature working inside the social texture of achieved levels. Character is a vitality that originates from the Being, ready to comprehend all alone, be eager all alone and be a pioneer for the general public. Regardless of whether the field is in writing, or logical revelation or in industry or in establishing a school, this is the fundamental distinction among character and character.

What are the prerequisites of character and character? Character ca exclude character, however, a character must incorporate the limits of character and not be constrained by them. Character requires understanding, quality of will, constancy, and vitality. Thoughts are potential, amazing and bolstered by the general public. The limit with respect to the brain to follow up on a thought gives you character. All men of high character will have solid, great assessments. Be that as it may, the comprehension of character is constrained in light of the fact that it sees just what every other person has comprehended.

Psyche acts as indicated by fixed propensities and inclinations. There are incredible men of extremely high character. Their inclination is consistently for refined living and their propensities are acceptable propensities. Their psychological developments are of an elevated level of achievement. In any case, they are bound by their conclusions.

What character requires is unadulterated understanding, autonomous of a subsequent individual. The general blessings of character are unadulterated insight in the psyche, warmth, and extensiveness in the heart, dynamism in the imperative, continuance and tirelessness in the physical. In the event that these things are there all alone, they will incorporate all the limits of character. For character, the limit of the brain to take a plan to a hopeful level, for the accomplishment of the perfect is the place it contrasts from character. A man with a character will be liberal. He won't be bound by his suppositions or have unbending inclinations. He will lean toward what is best at that point and be eager to change his propensities if vital.

To summarize, the unadulterated segments of character are:

- In the brain - common sense, lucidity, understanding;
- In the will - dauntlessness and balance;
- In the heart - preservation, warmth, extensiveness, and attraction;
- In the indispensable - vitality;
- In the physical - determination and continuance for work.

Some of the time character deteriorates into character, or character develops into character in a similar individual. An individual may have a character in an organization, yet not in governmental issues. Individuals who have established banks, or schools, or little organizations, or individuals who have chosen to move away from their nation to another nation are individuals who have a character at that level. All individuals who are dependable to their families, to their youngsters, to their folks, who satisfy certain degrees of achievement substantially, who are simply, reasonable, and moral, have moral characters, social characters, physical characters.

For the most part, the character is comprehended to be something acceptable. Be that as it may, it tends to be negative moreover. A dealer has a character just as an individual from the Mafia. Be that as it may, his character doesn't communicate in a positive way. He realizes how to sort out individuals and how to be faithful to his gathering. He certainly has character. An individual who has character will have individuals around him. An individual of insignificant behavior won't draw in adherents.

Individuals who state, "Mention to me what I ought to do and I will do it" are at the degree of behavior. They can get things done, they can obey individuals, they can eat what is served, however, they can't deal with others. Individuals who state, "Give me this work and I will achieve it and report back to you," have a character at that level. Others who state, "Let me look at this proposition and if my psyche comprehends and favors, my feelings will be enthused and I can follow up on my own," have character.

Behavior is the outer appearance without being affirmed or bolstered by the brain and sentiments. Character is what is bolstered by the psyche and sentiments. It is behavior that is supported and coordinated by the brain. Character is all alone. It is self-coordinated.

Chapter 3

COMMUNICATION SKILLS

All that we do impacts others, even without our knowing or significance. The writers of such books utilize this reality to contend: since we as of now do this, why not does it so to increase some profit? In an article around one of those pervasive "get craftsmen", I read, in addition to other things, his remark that there are manners by which a man may energize the lady he wants to be progressively fearless, or that by utilizing explicit words he can propose that she is unconstrained, has a brave soul, is loose, and so forth and that there is nothing negative about this.

Relational abilities are unimaginably significant in human relations in light of the fact that with indiscreet correspondence we can make various false impressions and issues. Frequently, however, there is a meager line between the cognizant utilization of specialized techniques to improve connections, and to impact individuals to do things we need them to do, yet which maybe are not what they genuinely need to do, or when they are not by any means mindful of our expectations.

For instance, guardians who use correspondence procedures with their kids regularly don't utilize them in a fair endeavor to comprehend what their kids need and feel, yet to manipulation their conduct, in the previous case of temptation workshops, such strategies are utilized to get sex or have a short throw without uncovering one's actual goals, and particularly without considering conceivable passionate and physical ramifications for a lady. They may likewise be utilized to get the other individual to go gaga for you before they have gotten an opportunity to find a good pace better and can decide what amount they truly like you. Moreover, men in those workshops were urged to cause a lady to feel uncertain and increment her craving to satisfy desires.

What is "acceptable" for other people?

Advertisers of the utilization of the craft of correspondence to manipulation others would state that we really benefit them, specifically in the event that we prevail with regards to making the other individual truly need to carry on in the manner we need or to rest easy thinking about themselves. This thought, be that as it may, is an ill-bred mentality and suggests that we realize what is useful for the other individual better than they know. This is a self-absorbed and youthful methodology in some cases even in a parent - youngster relationship, and particularly according to another grown-up. Regardless of whether you attempt to keep someone from committing an error - individuals need botches. By what another method would we be able to learn, if not for a fact?

Regardless of whether we accept we are doing acceptable to the next, we need to inquire as to whether we can truly feel better and have an unmistakable inner voice realizing that we have affected someone else without their insight? Is it conceivable to do this with a genuine regard for the other, in the event that we through deliberate manipulation put them in the situation of a more vulnerable, manipulated individual? In such a relationship genuineness and closeness are not prone to happen. From another viewpoint, is it at all conceivable to impact someone else with their full information and understanding, on the off chance that we regularly don't have any acquaintance with ourselves how we impact others?

Maybe the more you attempt to avoid the other individual that you are attempting to impact them, the more you attempt to do this from a discourteous position. Specialized strategies are the most legitimate and deferential in the event that we can apply them without concealing our aims. I for one, for my own respectability, favor approaches that are not intended to stir explicit feelings or reactions, yet to push someone else to intentionally and freely consider their own and my perspectives.

What is the genuine reason?

The requirement for power is inside all individuals. We want to sparkle, to be alluring to other people, to feel amazing; for all individuals, these are extremely appealing pictures and it's anything but difficult to legitimize our endeavors to accomplish them. The inquiry we once in a while consider is the reason do we want to do this? What sort of feeling is missing inside that makes us look for consolation in such a way? For what reason do we feel commendable enough just when we feel unique or superior to other people?

Chipping away at our own sentiments of confidence (and on our innovativeness) instead of on an outside picture may spare us years as well as many years of exertion.

Additionally, no sort of outside progress can change the manner in which we feel about ourselves, with the exception of incidentally. Confidence must originate from inside as opposed to from without. At that point, it's an inclination that is exceptionally superior to manipulation over others. At the point when you have sound confidence, you will in all probability demonstrate such that will inspire others to esteem and love you more profound than you could accomplish utilizing any kind of craftiness.

Perceive manipulation

When in doubt, on the off chance that you feel quietly manipulated in a discussion with somebody, regardless of whether you don't see how - it's conceivable valid. For all intents and purposes, any correspondence ability can be utilized deceptively. The key is the goal and the disposition of the other individual, while their outside conduct may be hard to perceive as manipulative. However, it's practically difficult to play that game without minor non-verbal signs giving us out: unpretentious changes in tonality, expanded unbending nature, little incoherency or absence of suddenness - things that individuals most likely won't notice deliberately, yet unwittingly they will.

In such a case, normally there is a natural inclination, something like "something feels unusual about this, yet I don't know what". The sooner you recognize and investigate that feeling, the better (yet to have the option to make it rapidly, rather when it's past the point of no return, you have to practice watching your sentiments.) To abstain from being manipulated, frequently it's a smart thought to state to the next individual that you need some an opportunity to think, for instance on the off chance that someone is requesting some help. Particularly in the event that you are being convinced to make a buy, say that you'll be back after you have thought about it, head outside, go for a stroll and ponder the choice without outer impact.

Manipulation vs. healthy self-esteem

It's such a great amount of simpler to live with trustworthiness, rather than having to continually manipulation ourselves and imagine something we don't generally feel; continually stressing on the off chance that we missed something or in the event that someone may see through our demonstration, okay truly need to put such a great amount of vitality into manipulation, regardless of whether you felt that there were no different issues the longing to manipulation individuals may be demonstrating?

You may be playing a transient game, which implies you are most likely mindful that you don't generally think about the other individual. Another chance is that you need to keep individuals around you intrigued constantly (want to have mystique) to have the option to feel significant or amazing. Right now, to other people, just as irreverence to your own self, maybe oblivious - an inward feeling of not being commendable or significant enough, which is secured by endeavors to manipulation others? An individual without solid confidence will be pulled in to strategies, books, and workshops offering force and magnetism, wanting to fill the internal void made by an oblivious conviction that their actual self and legit sentiments can't draw in affection and appreciation.

Enticement

I've referenced enticement techniques before. Frequently, some enticement techniques are utilized as normal and even anticipated "mating ceremonies": being a tease, blessings, underlining physical properties, praises... Sometimes, the enticer may be actually intrigued, and some of the time childishly, yet since the conduct is the equivalent, it may be hard to recognize one from the other. The "tempted" individual should accept that the enticer was straightforward, might appreciate the consideration and positive sentiments. Such individuals may trust that the "tempter" is utilizing such cliché conduct since it's a typical and commonplace approach to be sentimental.

Now and again it is along these lines, yet I would state that the more regular and unconstrained one is in communicating their sentimental emotions, the almost certain it is that they are straightforward and open in different everyday issues and that they have sound confidence which permits them to act naturally. As an extra assistance in evaluating potential love intrigue, see how they speak with individuals who are not all that significant in their lives. At the point when the sentiment wears off, they will most likely treat you likewise.

Ramifications for the manipulator

At the point when you use relational abilities, inquire as to whether you're utilizing them to shroud your actual goals and sentiments, or to communicate them in a proper way. Each time we use relational abilities to abstain from being straightforward and open, we likewise dismiss our own actual self and an opportunity to acknowledge ourselves. Likewise, later on, it will be progressively hard to regard yourself, knowing how you utilized individuals without thinking about results they would endure.

The cost of counterfeit manipulation over others – regardless of whether we figure out how to accomplish it – is that we would never unwind and act naturally. We'd be feeling the squeeze to continue supporting the deception, involved with others, however ourselves as well. We'd be continually cautious and stressing if the others may at long last transparent us. What the writers of every one of those books on allure and Persuasion won't let you know is that having authority over others presumes a lot of more regrettable, excruciating command over yourself, over the legitimate and solid pieces of you. Maybe there are hardly any better instances of the "boomerang – impact" than the techniques for manipulating others.

On the off chance that you are enticed to attempt this sort of games, ask yourself: do you need loose, unconstrained associations with solid individuals who wouldn't endure such games, individuals who see you and value you as you are – or would you like to consider individuals to be manikins, attempt to shape them into what you want, and along these lines pull in youthful individuals who acknowledge games and affectation, who couldn't see you and love you in the event that you were yourself?

At whatever point I met individuals who manipulated others, regardless of whether they had to prevail with regards to accomplishing some force and impact over others, I never felt that they were extremely upbeat, truly enjoying and valuing themselves. The cost of being an effective manipulator is that others may like, perhaps appreciate, your demonstration, a bogus projection, yet not your actual self. Unexpectedly, it's simply a similar demeanor you originate from, and the more you prevail in manipulation, the more troublesome it is to perceive and transform it. The value you pay is your confidence, in light of the fact that, regardless of the amount you deny or legitimize it, you realize you cheat individuals. Then again, I've likewise met individuals who emanate genuine magnetism. Their engaging quality originates from solid confidence – tolerating what their identity is and making the most of their reality.

7 Cs Of Effective Communication

There are 7 important points which can make your ordinary communication a very effective communication.

COMPLETENESS will bring the desired response

Completeness means that whatever you communicate should be complete and there should be no missing facts in your speech. It is often seen that people assume some facts to be known by the audience or listeners. This is not the right approach because if you started to assume this then, you will not be able to give the whole details of the core objective. The whole idea will become confused and you will be facing troubles in making other understand.

You should provide very detailed information to your listeners and in fact you should try to provide some additional information to make your points clearer. While preparing your presentation or report, you should make sure that you are answering all possible questions which your topic can have.

In this way, audience will be more understanding about your topic and they will ask you more logical questions. It often happens that after you finish your presentation in office then, someone says, "What are you actually trying to say." This is probably worst comment that you can get after a tiring presentation but you should think over again that why someone said that. There will be some flaws in your presentation or some confusing factors which have urged that person to say so. To avoid such embarrassing situations, you should try to make your presentation clearer and complete without ignoring any fact and mentioning even very minor details.

Completeness brings the desired response from the receiver or listener or your audience. You need to include everything which you think is related to your topic of discussion and try to describe both positive and negative approaches.

CONCISENESS will save time

Conciseness is another important aspect of effective communication and especially when you talk about business communication then, you should know that your message should be very concise because this will make it more proper, to the point and time saving to understand. Time is very important in modern day life and no one has the time to listen to you for full hour while you can deliver the same meaning and discussion in 30 minutes.

Besides, if you add unnecessary pause, repeat information and use other similar tactics to prolong the duration then, your audience will get bore and they will prefer to either leave the discussion or they will stop taking interest.

You should only include very relevant facts about your topic and avoid using unnecessary information to be added for example if you are making a presentation for the annual budget of your organization then, you should keep thing to the point and void giving irrelevant examples for cutting down the budget or increasing it.

Your aim is to present report of your annual budget and this does not mean that you should add suggestions because that is associated to someone else. If you tried to over express yourself then, it may happen that you will confuse your audience with wordy expressions and there will be lots of discussion, which people will never understand due to broken language. So make your information concise and save time for yourself as well as for your audience.

CONSIDERATION means understanding of human nature

Consideration is one of the most important things in effective communication because it will make sure that you understand the receiver in a better way. When you say consider then, this means, you have to think twice about certain things and make sure that you are always conveying your message in a positive tone. Even if there are some negative points in your discussion then, you should try to overcome those by emphasizing on positive points.

In proper and effective consideration, it is important to understand that the more you explain benefits, more interesting your discussion will become. So you should try to explain each and every benefit of your discussion which will make people more attentive and they will be more interested in integrating those benefits in their lives. Try to focus more on "you" instead of 'I" or "We". This also sends a very pleasant impression that you actually care more about others instead of yourself.

There is a saying that thinks before you speak and this saying completes the part of consideration. You should properly analyze everything before presenting it to others. Analyze everything from receiver's point of view because that will allow you to think about those questions which are often neglected by following just one approach. You should never use negative expressions like I hate instead replace them with I prefer.

Similarly there are so many replacement which you can make and avoid all the negativity from your discussion. If you have to say confident then, you can say unstoppable, fortunate can be replaced with blessed because these words also have a positive meaning but the replacement are even greater.

CONCRETENESS reinforces confidence

Concreteness means that you should be very specific and accurate about the facts and figures which you represent in your discussion. The fact should be very clear and being accurate is even more important because people often give value of words and especially figures which you represent. Verb choice should also be very vivid and defined and wording should be such that it should create a very positive image of your overall topic. If you start to sound little vague, obscure and general about the facts then, things will start to get confusing and people will start to think negatively. Emphasis on one thing will be lost and as a result the effectiveness of communication will not be present.

If you are presenting some solid and true facts and figures then, it will automatically boost your confidence. You should try to gather figures from different surveys and internet can be a very good place to do this research. No matter what kind of topic you have but you will find things related to that topic and in all formats.

You can give people's opinion about your topic and then see how your audience responds. But you should remember one thing that all the facts and figures should be specific and related to your core topic and they should not be irrelevant.

CLARITY can make things more comprehensive

Clarity is often mistaken by people and they think that making the fact more clear is clarity but clarity is more about making your speech and exact message better. You need to choose your words more precisely and use simpler language to convey your message. Simpler you language will be, easier it will be for the audience to decode your message easily and they will get hold of your idea very clearly. Best way to bring clarity is to use simpler words and make simple and easy to understand paragraphs. Do not try to be too formal with the choice of words and try to remain casual in approach.

If you tried to be too formal in your approach and used too heavy language then, it is a known fact that not everyone can understand the heavy and complex language. Especially these days' people are really weak in their language and formal language has been reserved only for news and newspaper columns.

Normal people understand just normal and simple language and it is best way to convey your message in its exact and raw form. As it is mentioned in the heading that clarity makes your message more comprehensive and this is true because if you use fewer words then, it will be easier for the receiver to receive and decode the message and he will get precise meaning of message very easily.

On the other hand, if you made the whole message confuse by adding unnecessary and heavy words in it then, ultimately, you will be able to convey half of the message while the other half will be lost in those heavy words. So make your message as clear as possible and try to use fewer and simpler words in it so that everyone can understand it.

COURTASY makes relations stronger

Courtesy means that you should some respect to the receiver. Especially when it comes to business communication then, you message should start with a respectful word and should end on a respectful clause as well. This is just a way of giving value to the feeling of the receiver. Your choice of words can depict the courtesy and you should be very thoughtful in choosing words. Always think about the caliber of the audience and if you are giving presentations to your boss then, it add even more responsibility. Always use nondiscriminatory expressions because these expressions will convince the other person that you always value their thoughts.

If you are being appreciative, thoughtful, and respectful and using polite words and gestures then, the receiver will feel good about your discussion and will start to take interest in your discussion even more. You can take a simple example that if some mail comes to you which is starting from simple hi, hello then, you will not value it a lot but if same email comes with saying hi our respectful and valued customer then, you will definitely try to look into it. These are some things which show professionalism of people.

CORRECTNESS will avoid all the confusion

To be correct, you should be aware and awareness means that you should target right audience. You should know the social, educational and religious background of the reader or audience and then, use your language according to that background. If you start to address labor in the same way as you address a CEO then, things will start to get confusing for that person.

This does not mean that you should not respect labors as you give to CEO but this means there should be a different level of respect for both of these persons and you should follow certain protocols, use right language, avoid punctuation errors, use precise and accurate information. All of these features will make your communication more correct and more effective.

If you start to make your language ambiguous and improper or you have too many punctuation and grammar mistakes then, people will not value your message and in the end, it will be added as ineffective communication. But you can change this very easily by adding some true facts and figures and keeping your grammar simple and correct.

Now these are all the 7 Cs of communication and if you can learn to control all seven of them, then, you will have a very effective communication method. In short you can say that if your message is concise, complete, considered, correct, clear, courteous and concrete then, it is said to be an effective message.

Becoming A Great Communicator From A Good Communicator

You will have many employees in your office whom you see and you think that "they must have always been like this" well this is not true for all of them because communication needs certain set of rules and every good communicator has to follow them.

It may happen that people whom you see may have got these principles so effectively integrated that they do not even think about them anymore but they just act on those principals but at some point time in the past, they must have gone through same phase from which you are going through. So you need to take courage and select a path, there are so many thing which you can do to enhance your communication and in this discussion, I am going to illustrate some of them.

An interpersonal communication skill, as it is evident from these words that are very personal but all of such skills are purely learned. There are so many concrete things which can integrate some very effective interpersonal communication skills in your personality. You just need to make yourself ready and be ready to take this challenge to improve yourself as a whole.

COMMIT YOURSELF TO IMPROVE

Like all other skill learning processes, you should commit yourself to learn these skills and make sure that there is nothing in your mind which can distract you from your plan. If you can make such a concrete commitment then, you can always improve your interpersonal skills to make progress in your filed.

You must keep your eyes on the overall progress and advantage which this skill will give you and this will keep you going on same path of improvement.

TRAINING IS IMPORTANT

There are different training programs for improving your interpersonal skills. You can be a part of these programs either join some of online programs or try to attend regular classes of such courses. People often think that these courses are just a way of making money and if you also think that these are just money making tactics then, you should look for some free courses.

There are numerous free courses available and you can roll in these courses to try your luck and improve your interpersonal skills. They will not charge you anything but will give you some of the very important and necessary training.

DEVELOPMENT SHOULD BE MONITORED

If you have been trying to improve your interpersonal communication skills then, you must also monitor your development. In order to make your skills better and enhanced, you should try to compare yourself and calculate the difference. People's opinion is the best way to go about because they will give you a realistic view of your communication skills.

Learn To Use Terms That Invoke Emotions

For most, the effective impacts desired out of a communicating exercise, comes from the importance of being able to invoke some level of emotion both from the presenter and the listener.

If the communication is well designed, with this important aspect dominantly featured, then the eventual results of the said communication exercise will bring forth the desired effects.

Learning how to identify and include terms in the speech pattern and body language will be very useful when trying to focus in invoking some sort of emotion from all involved.

Using appropriate trigger works and phrases is one way of achieving this emotional impact. "Painting" a picture with the choice of words used is the main idea behind the emotion invoking communication technique.

This is very important for the presenter who is focused on making the desired impact on the listener in order to get the results intended. However it should be also noted that the use of invoking emotions can be something that causes the opposite of the intended impact meant. Therefore it is very important to identify beforehand the emotions that are being sought after, through the communication exercise, so that the words chosen will rightly describe the actual content of the message intended to be divulged.

The following are some recommendations as to the best use of words that will ideally invoke emotions:

- Using descriptive words and visual words to make it easy for the listener to "see" the picture in the mind's eye would be one way of invoking the desired emotions.

- Using smiles and metaphors is another effective way of invoking the desired emotions into the content of the message to make it more impactful.

- There are also actual words that can be used to invoke strong emotions both in the presentation material and in the overall content intention.

Learn To Use Terms That Spark Interest

Any tools that can be used to enhance the communication exercise are definite exploring for its merits. Besides the more common recommendations such as body language and vocal tones, there is another equally interesting way to create optimum interest in the subject being communicated. This is the art of incorporating little nuggets of information that can spark the interest of the listener.

When it comes to perking the interest of the listener, the most common way to spark interest is to name drop. This has always been a crowd puller because by nature most people are rather inquisitive and want to know all about what others are doing or thinking. Therefore by name dropping the conversation now becomes more interesting and thus worth the time and effort to indulge in. Giving out information that is attention grabbing is also another form of sparking the interest of the listener through the communication exercise.

Using facts and figures that create or imply shocking information that is little know, will add to the excitement levels of the communication content, thus encouraging and sparking even more interest.

Another way to help spark interest is to be well informed in the subject matter that is being discussed. People are often attracted to individuals who are well informed on the topic of discussion.

Projecting a seemingly commanding presence by the tone of voice and the topic chosen for discussion is also another way to spark interest from those around. Presentations that are made with voice tones and body language that personifies confidence will ideally create a resonance that attracts interest.

Using terms that are positive and encourage interaction is always a welcomed way to ensure participation, and this if often the ingredient that encourages interest. Most people enjoy some form of interactive conversations as it allows them to ask questions and engage with others.

Improve Your Communication Skills, Become A Better Listener

Listening, often overlooked, is a vital aspect of the human communication process. While speaking is often practiced and emphasized by many, the art of listening isn't one on which we find people spending much effort. In actuality, listening is easy and can be improved by following just a few simple steps.

Being a good listener means that everything you hear comes directly from the speaker and not from your interpretation of their words. This means that, as the speaker is talking, you are listening to the words as they are being spoken instead of trying to guess the point that the speaker is trying to make. People are often guilty of jumping to conclusions when they do this and, in doing so, they disrupt their listening ability. When jumping to conclusions, the person often doesn't hear the speaker's message because it is blocked out by his or her own assumptions. Good listeners absorb all of the information while the words are being spoken and avoid thinking ahead and forming their own conclusions.

Giving the speaker your undivided attention is probably one of the most important tips to good communication. Concentrate on the speaker's words and avoid tuning out their message. When speaking on the phone, many people engage in other activities such as reading newspapers, checking email and other activities that can distract from the conversation. Many listeners zone out during face-to-face situations by either thinking about their response to the speaker or by daydreaming about something completely unrelated to the subject.

When you allow yourself to be distracted, your listening skills are not what they need to be. Missing a critical point of the speaker's presentation can be the result of just a small amount of distraction. If you can focus your attention completely on the speaker, you will hear all that is being said. In addition, you can ensure that you are being a good listener and are taking in all of the pertinent information.

One technique of being a better listener involves creating mental images of the speaker's words. This is a way of visualization that allows you to really comprehend the words you are hearing. These visualization skills can enhance the way that people process information. By using these mental images, you will help yourself by retaining the information you have just heard. This enhanced and improved comprehension makes you a better listener.

Taking care to note your body language can be another way to be a good listener. You will offend your listener if you engage in body language that lets the speaker feel that he or she is not being listened to. Behaviors such as avoiding eye contact, crossing your arms or wincing can send a message to a speaker that you are not really listening to them. These types of body language or mannerisms can result in the conversation being cut short because the speaker does not feel you are interested in what they are saying.

You can also consider asking questions that relate to the speaker's statements. This technique can also help you to become a better listener. Remember to ask questions without allowing your questions to interfere with your listening ability. If you find yourself focusing on one of the speaker's key points and spending the rest of the conversation trying to think of a question that addresses that point, you will miss a lot of information. Instead, try asking your questions immediately when you think of them. This way, you can have your question answered in the context of the speaker's presentation without having it affect your listening abilities. When you ask questions as part of listening, it allows the speaker to recognize that his or her presentation is being followed and that you are interested in learning more about the topic.

If you practice your listening skills, you will be well on your way to becoming a better listener. Try making a conscientious effort to use your listening skills each time you speak to someone or participate in a presentation. Remain completely focused on the conversation or presentation and try not to guess what the speaker is going to say. Create mental images of the words being spoken and ask valid questions to confirm what you have just heard. Each time you have the opportunity to listen, try to work on these important listening skills.

While listening is not as widely practiced as speaking in the art of conversation, it is just as important. When you are an excellent listener, you will not only ensure that you are receiving information but will assure the speaker that you care about the information being presented and that you understand their message.

The Science of Charisma

The study of charisma and its role in leadership began Max Weber. The pioneering sociologist who lived from 1864 until 1920 defined charismatic leadership as gifted, inspired motivation from a leader who pursues a vision which attracts followers to identify with and emulate him.

Charismatic leaders have strong core values that drive their behavior. They are also articulate, with the ability to speak dynamically, forcefully, and so persuasively that other people to buy into the vision, and to want to achieve it. They are generally unconventional trailblazers; self-confident, and with a sufficient amount of competence that people feel comfortable following their lead. This makes charisma especially important in a crisis situation because people are more likely to look toward a person who appears capable of bringing them through.

Professor of psychology Howard Friedman (University of California-Riverside) is a specialist in non-verbal communication. He defines charisma as "a certain presence."

When charismatic people enter a room, their mere presence draws attention and their energy may radiate to enliven the entire gathering. At the core of this charisma, says Friedman, is "a basic self-confidence" and the ability to project this to others.

Right now, you're at a fork in the road. Will you continue doing the same-old thing with the same old results, or will you move forward in a new direction...one that may seem a little scary at first...in order to make your life fuller, more successful, and more joyful?

I expect you may need a small "push" to get you going in the right direction because the fact of the matter is: Your charisma quotient needs to be improved...and that takes work!

You have to commit yourself mentally to doing whatever is necessary to raise your charisma quotient. Here's a list of "oldies, but goodies"...an overview of the amazing things that having charisma can do for you!

1 You'll get far more respect than the average

person!

2 People will be drawn to you without any effort on your part!

3 You'll exude self-confidence!

4 You'll seem powerful without being intimidating.

5 You'll put people at ease and make them feel understood!

6 And you'll be able to easily get what you want, because people will instinctively want to help you!

In your personal relationships, the quality of charisma can make your life fuller and more joyful. Members of your family and your friends will be far happier in your company, and you will have a greater influence on them, causing them to feel better about themselves and to do better at the important things in their lives.

Your charisma makes you irresistible, not only from the point of view of your communication skills.

Webster's Ninth New Collegiate Dictionary defines charisma as "a personal magic of leadership arousing special popular loyalty or enthusiasm for a public figure."

Charisma is also that special quality of magnetism that each person has and that each person uses to a certain degree. The people who look up to you, who respect and admire you, the members of your family and your friends and co-workers would probably say that they find you charismatic. Why? Because whenever one person feels a positive emotion towards another, he imbues that person with charisma!

In trying to explain charisma, some people speak of an "aura" that radiates out from a person and affects the people around him/her in a positive or negative way. You also have an aura around you that most people cannot see. But visible or not, it's there nevertheless. This aura affects the way people react and respond to you, either positively or negatively. So it's easy to see why it's in your very best interest to learn to control this aura and make it work to your advantage.

Charisma Sells

The charismatic salesperson is almost invariably a top performer in his field who enjoys all the rewards that go with superior sales. If you're in sales, your charisma can have a major impact on the way your prospects and customers treat you and deal with you. I'm sure you've noticed that top salespeople seem to be far more successful than the average salespeople in getting along with their customers.

Charismatic salespeople are always more welcome, more positively received and more trusted than the others. They sell more, and they sell more easily. They make a better living and they build better lives than people who have not fully developed their charisma potential. Salespeople with charisma get far more pleasure out of their work and suffer less stress and rejection.

Charisma Makes You Influential

If you're in business, developing greater charisma can help you tremendously in working with your staff, your suppliers, your bankers, your customers and everyone else upon whom you depend for your success.

People seem naturally drawn to those who possess charisma. When you've got charisma, other people will want to help you and support you in your success efforts. People will open doors for you and bring you opportunities that otherwise would not have been available to you.

Charisma gives you a tremendous advantage in almost every conceivable situation:

1 Sales calls or face-to-face
2 Business meetings
3 Getting your kids to do their homework
4 Enlisting the cooperation of a store clerk or teacher.

Just imagine how much easier your life will be when people are instantly drawn to you and automatically want to help you.

You'll be able to inspire people, ignite their enthusiasm, persuade them to see things your way, and do what you want them to—without creating defensiveness or resentment. That's the beauty of charisma! Charisma doesn't turn you into a crafty trickster, pulling the wool over people's eyes and fooling them. When you unleash your charisma - which is really just saying when you live and speak authentically, from a place of "inner truth" -- people will naturally want to be on your side.

Whether you're running a corporation, a department, a classroom, a volunteer program, or a household, there's no skill more valuable than the ability to positively influence others.

You already have the potential to be more charismatic. Together, we're going to unlock it, so you, too, can have an extraordinary edge in life shared only by a select few.

But What Is Charisma?

Dr. Tony Alessandra defines charisma as "the ability to influence others positively by connecting with them physically, emotionally, and intellectually."

He also quotes Harvard anthropologist Charles Lindholm's definition: "Charisma is, above all, a relationship, a mutual mingling of the inner selves of leader and follower."

Charisma - the real McCoy - has certain characteristics: expansiveness for instance and energy, joy and creativity. Charisma is a way of being which calls forth all your powers - from the pragmatic to the inspirational, the intellectual to the intuitional -- and a way of relating to yourself, to those you work with and play with - and even to the "universe" itself.

That is why at its core, charisma is both disarmingly simple and immeasurably complex -- it is the spirit which is unique to you.

Establishing contact with your unique spirit...learning to understand and to respect it...and finally having the courage to live from it is what gaining charisma is all about. The more fully and honestly your unique nature shows itself, the more charisma you will have. Simple? Nothing could be simpler.

You Are What You Speak - Charismatic Words

In discussions of charisma, most people immediately say "sex appeal" when asked to describe a characteristic of someone who is charismatic. But Cynthia Emrich, associate professor of management at the School of Business at the College of William and Mary, thinks otherwise. "If the (charismatic person) is attractive, but you don't have any clue [about where he or she stands] you can't identify with him. The leader loses potency."

Emrich grew interested in the language of charisma after reading a theory that memorable art creates images in the viewer's mind. A study of Shakespeare's sonnets, for example, found that the most popular sonnets had the most image-based words such as heart," hand" or "desert."

Emrich contends that in the pre-television era, words sometimes nosed out looks as the source of charisma. "We tend to equate charisma with a type of sex appeal or charm, but you can find charismatic leaders who were pretty darn unattractive," she says pointing to British Prime Minister Winston Churchill, unarguably tremendously charismatic, but not attractive physically.

There is no definite theory as to why image words would be more persuasive and charismatic than idea words, although some studies suggest that it's because they engage a different part of the brain. When you use image-based words, says Emrich, "it's not just something they see, but also hear and taste."

So an important part of charisma is the ability to elicit images in the mind of a follower. A message that is easy to "see" is easier to understand, and that works well for the message and the messenger.

The A-B-C Basics of Charismatic Communication

Communication Basic A - Let Your Voice Come From Deep Within You - Involving Your Body

It's more likely than not that you don't involve your body in your speaking very much. You probably take shallow breaths, and when you speak, the resonance of your voice probably comes mainly out of your throat, neck and head, rather than out of your chest or deeper in your body. Not good.

You must practice breathing more deeply, and practice letting sound come out of that deeper place within you.

Communication Basic B - Speak with Excitement

Many people who have been told that they lack charisma have usually gotten into the habit of never showing any real excitement about anything. Charismatic, attractive people, on the other hand, are good at conveying their enthusiasm about things in their lives by the way that they speak. You can learn to do this by practicing speaking excitedly about things.

Get so excited about something that the gauge explodes.

You do this by practice. Choose a topic, and spend one speaking about that topic with enthusiasm. Really let yourself go, and get excited about it! It doesn't matter if you're talking about baseball, a recipe for brownies, your spouse, your business, or world politics. The subject doesn't matter nearly as much as your ability to convey your excitement about it.

As you practice speaking excitedly, you'll find you are more animated and exciting in all your conversations. And this will make you much more charismatic.

Communication Basic C - Don't Be Wishy Washy

Many people who come across as boring and un-focused were not rewarded during their formative years for speaking with certainly or decisiveness. As a result, they've come to believe that the best way to get along in life was to stay "under the radar," and to never appear too committed to anything.

That's a good way to get along, okay, if you don't mind being completely devoid of charisma...and all the benefits that charisma brings. If you'd rather do more than just get along, if you'd like to really be charismatic in your personal and business life, it's time to start experimenting with speaking with certainty. The easiest way to stop appearing to be drifting without a rudder is to remove the words "I guess" from your vocabulary.

Tiny verbal changes can have a huge impact in how dynamic and charismatic you seem to other people. But "waste removal" is just half the task. When you break a habit (like saying "I guess"), you can't simply stop the behavior. You must replace one behavior with another.

When it comes to radiating charisma, you should remove all words of doubt and replace them with words of certainty.

1. Instead of saying, "I guess so," try saying, "Yes!"
2. Instead of saying "I guess that'd be okay," try saying, "That's what I want."
3. Instead of saying, "I guess we could sit over there," try saying, "Let's sit over there."

Some people have natural charisma in their speaking. The rest of us just have practice.

The 13 Different Faces of Charisma

Who's Got the Power (of Charisma)...and Why Author Doe Lang has written extensively about charisma and has identified 13 different instances where charisma is exhibited:

1. **Cross-Over Charisma** - the charisma that people gain from achieving success in one area can cross-over with them to a completely different area of endeavor.

   Example: charismatic actor/bodybuilder Arnold Schwarzenegger crossed-over into California politics much like predecessor Ronald Reagan.

2. **Cumulative Charisma** - People, particularly celebrities, who spend many, many years of achievement in the public eye become so iconic that their charisma transcends whatever their current situation might be.

   Example: This is particularly evident in "fallen idols" like Elvis and Marilyn Monroe.

3. **Intellectual Charisma** - Philosophers, writers, and the world's great thinkers were magnetic thanks to the power of their ideas, as well as their ability to convey them. This also applies to people who are successful in business

   Example: Einstein, Thomas Wolfe, Maureen Dowd

4. **Intrinsic Charisma** - This is the most elusive of all forms of charisma. It's the thing that makes someone "my most unforgettable person." It has nothing to do with fame or fortune, and often is found in the most simple person. This charisma can't be learned and is truly a gift from the universe.

   Examples: a clergyman, your 5th grade music teacher, a Holocaust survivor

5. **Legendary (also called "mythic") Charisma -** Truly the stuff legends are made of, this charisma is ascribed to real and fictional characters whose larger-than-life achievements make them enormously appealing:

   Examples: Columbus, Goliath, Paul Bunyon, etc.

6. **Media Charisma -** You need look no further than television reality series to see the power of the media in making someone charismatic. Everyday people whose only achievement is to be seen on television suddenly become sought-after...especially as commercial spokespeople so they can cash-in on their "15 minutes" of charisma.

   Example: Omarosa (The Apprentice)

7. **Money Charisma -** Nothing is as alluring as power, unless it's the money that buys that power. For many, all it takes is money charisma to turn a "weirdo" into an "eccentric" or an "ugly" person into someone with "a unique personal style."

   Example: Bill Gates, Donald Trump,

8. **Performance Charisma** - Unlike performance anxiety, performance charisma is a good thing. It doesn't matter if you're the biggest star in the Hollywood firmament, or the under-paid, over-worked keyboard player in a local bar band, your role as a performer immediately gives you charismatic appeal. (Hey, didn't you ever hear of groupies!)

Example: Billy Bob Thornton, Sean Penn, Oprah Winfrey,

9. **Political Charisma** - Also known as Power Charisma, political charisma ebbs and flows along with the success of the politician. A newly elected President is dripping with political charisma, but is likely to watch it start to erode the minute he makes a decision that's unpopular with constituents.

   Example: Colin Powell, Bill Clinton, Margaret Thatcher

10. **Scientific Charisma** - The ability to uncover new facts, discover new worlds, and cure old ills makes scientists highly charismatic. We want to know more about them and how they think so that we can think big thoughts, too.

    Example: NASA scientists, Jonas Salk

11. **Situational Charisma** - Some people are lucky enough to be born into a life that gives them charisma. Royal, political, and celebrity offspring often enjoy carry-over charisma thanks to their parents' status, but frequently squander their charisma "capital" by behaving badly.

    Example: Princess Diana, Paris Hilton

12. **Spiritual Charisma -** The magnetic charisma of ancient religious figures and more contemporary leaders comes from their spiritual faith and selfless devotion to their belief system.

Example: Jesus, Buddha, Mother Teresa,

13. **Sports Charisma** - The cult of personality around famous sports stars - call it "charisma by scorecard" - is huge. Madison Avenue leverages that charisma by having well-loved sports figures pitch products so consumers will be eager to emulate their charismatic idol and "Be like Mike."

Example: Michael Jordan, Serena Williams, Cristiano Ronaldo.

Can Charisma Be Measured?

Can charisma be measured? Yes, an examination of nonverbal cues such as facial expressions, gestures and body movements speak volumes about someone's charisma.

For example, charismatic people smile naturally, with wrinkling around the eyes. They are generally demonstrative, often touch friends during conversations. Even people who may be characterized as shy may also be considered charismatic and influential because of their ability to transmit emotions through nonverbal cues. Inscrutable people are the opposite pole and are the least charismatic.

Can Charisma Be Learned?

Despite appearances to the contrary, charisma is not a mysterious, indefinable character trait, but an inter-connected set of skills.   Some people learn these skills when they're young because were lucky enough to learn by example - from their parents, a teacher, a member of the clergy, etc. Charisma can be developed; it is not product of DNA and genetics. The expression, "Leaders are made, not born" and the corollary "Charisma is nurture, not nature" is a staple of the personal and executive coaching industry.

Okay, so you're probably asking: "If a person can learn to become more charismatic, what are the foundational steps to achieving personal charisma?"

Changing your Charisma Quotient from "Okay" to "Oh my goodness!" is simply a matter of developing the secret skills listed below:

1 **Secret Skill #1 - "Reading" People**
   In order to communicate with someone, you'll want to have a sense of what they're thinking and feeling. You can acquire this skill by observing people you know during the, trying to guess what emotion they are feeling, and then asking them if your guess is correct.

2 **Secret Skill #2 - Emotional Expression**
Studies have shown that most people are not nearly as good at communicating emotion non-verbally as they think they are. How do you do it? With **the tone of your voice, your face, and your body language**.

The best way to improve your emotional expression is to try to convey more feeling when you're conversing with people. If you want to improve quickly, **practice in front of a mirror** or a video camera.

3 **Secret Skill #3 - Hiding Emotion (Selectively)**
Showing the wrong emotion at the wrong time can cause discomfort in others or make people lose respect for you (having no emotional control is a sign of immaturity and lack of self-discipline).

Some people are not very good at hiding their emotions from others. Their inability to seem neutral makes them **less charisma** because sometimes the unintentionally or intentionally expressed emotion is inappropriate to the situation.

4 **Secret Skill #4 - Learning to Read Between the Lines**
The best way to practice is to simply sit in a café and brush up on your people-watching. Observe passers-by during their verbal and non-verbal interactions with one another and look for subtle clues and signals they may be giving off

5 Secret Skill #5- Playing by the (Social) Rules

When in Rome, do as the Romans...if you want them to think you're charismatic. Social rules are different for different cultures, subcultures, ages, regions, etc.

Since part of being charismatic is "mirroring" what's going on around you (to make people feel comfortable with you), you need to pay attention, study, and ask questions to figure out what's considered "the norm" in a specific environment -- things like who goes through the door first, how to introduce yourself to others, who reports to whom, etc.

6 Secret Skill #6 - Develop a Multiple Personality

The ability to **play different roles with different people** and knowing what works best with different people is a tremendous boost to your Charisma Quotient. But if being charismatic is about being yourself, how can you play different roles and still be true to yourself?

Everyone's personality has many aspects. You're not always happy are you? Or always sad. You're not always friendly and you're not always outgoing, but you're not always a quiet loner either. Being socially flexible is about allowing the aspect of you that is **appropriate to a situation** to come out.

7 Secret Skill #7 - Talk the Talk

This is the ability to use words to express yourself clearly and interestingly. You can improve your skill by **paying attention to what**

makes some people interesting and others boring, and by practicing what you learn.

8 **Secret Skill #8 - Increase Your Word Power (Vocabulary)**
Spending more time expressing yourself verbally is very important — conversing, giving speeches — simply try to improve your ability to express yourself with words.

You don't have to memorize a new list of "20-dollar words" every morning, but trying to find different ways to express yourself is important.

And If you SHARE these secrets, people will find you more charismatic than ever!

Charisma and Leadership

People ascribe the quality of charisma to those leaders whom they feel can most enable them to achieve important goals or objectives. In a leadership role, your charisma shows itself as extraordinary performance and a focus on achieving extraordinary results. The results you achieve serve as a charismatic inspiration to others to perform at equally exceptional levels. Remember that charisma always comes from working on yourself, not trying to make others see you in a certain way. It comes from liking and accepting yourself unconditionally and doing your best to do and say the specific things that develop within you a powerful, charismatic personality. But we will see it better in the next chapter dedicated to the art of leadership.

Public Speaking Tips

Most people in the business at some point or another will be in a situation where public speaking is part of the promotional exercise of the business connection. Public speaking is not necessarily directed to just a large audience, as it can also be addressed to a smaller group of people. The idea behind the public speaking exercise is to be able to present information in an interesting and informative way.

The following are some tips as to what an individual attempting to engage in a public speaking exercise should focus on:

Public speaking requires a certain level of conviction to be incorporated into the general delivery of the material being presented.

This aura of conviction is the element that is going to connect with the receiving party to create the interest in the material being presented.

Besides the interest element, a presentation given with conviction will also encourage the listener to be more convinced and this effectively ensures the conversion to loyal customer bases.

Public speaking is more effective if done without having to read from prepared notes. Besides the probability of the material read out being less than engaging, there is also the danger of not being able to connect with the audience as the presenter is too busy reading the said material.

Maintaining eye contact is perhaps one of the more important elements to pay attention to and ensure that it is constantly practiced.

Without the ever important eye contact there is little chance of the presenter being able to hold the attention of the audience for long.

Even with exciting material being presented the eye contact element is necessary as it also gives the presenter a chance to gauge the receptiveness of the audience towards the material being presented.

This would help the presenter make the necessary on the spot adjustments to ensure the negative effect is not continuous.

But how Bad Communication Damages Your Business?

Regardless of the size of the business endeavor, bad communications can have a very negative impact on the said business and sometimes the impact is so detrimental that the eventual results may be almost impossible to correct. Therefore it is important to acknowledge that bad communication should be curbed or even eliminated at all costs.

The following are some areas that can be affected by bad communications:

A company's production levels can be severely affected by the use of bad communications, as this leads to a breakdown in communications and also productivity. When this happens, goals and deadlines are usually jeopardized.

Bad communications, can also lead to poor morale among the workers, which will also eventually spill over into the general business platform. Not understanding what is expected, thus performing below expectations will contribute to a lot of confusion and stagnation within the company's processes, which in turn will negatively impact the daily progress anticipated.

Mistakes are very common because of poor or bad communication skills of those issuing orders. In some cases this makes the already existing bad communications become even worse as the blaming exercise commences. Therefore it is very important to ensure all connected to a particular exercise understand all that is expected.

If poor communication still abound then there should be some form of readdress that can be encouraged to help overcome any negativity.

Chapter 4

THE INFLUENTIAL LEADER

The art of leadership

The art of leadership is sought by virtually everyone. It is claimed by many, defined by a few, and exercised by the unheralded, depending on the source you use. In fact, we know a lot about leadership; it is the application of leadership that creates confusion for most.

In spite of all the leadership texts, containing a veritable plethora of theories about leadership (each of which is THE KEY), leadership remains a very individual concept, exercised in many diverse yet successful ways. Indeed, successful application always results in leadership. Unsuccessful application is invariably counter-productive. So, is this another theory? No, but I will share with you some of my observations about where to look for leadership. It's my belief that although we may not be able to define it very precisely, we can recognize it when we see it.

We know that there are people called "formal leaders" and "informal leaders" in some of the literature. I am not going to talk about those "formal leaders," because they are by definition occupying positions of authority (i.e., a supervisory position) and that is their sole claim to leadership. "Informal leaders," on the other hand, exercise leadership from positions not formally designated for leadership, thus causing a problem for the organization. How the informal leader arises is curious, but it can often be caused by the lack of leadership in the "formal" position. But that doesn't mean that the "great man" theory takes place (that's the one that says when a crisis occurs and there's no one prepared to deal with it, someone will rise to the occasion and deal with it). Why is someone not in a leadership position given authority by the group in which they work to exercise leadership?

There are, of course, several answers to that question, so let's examine some of them. It may be that the one who is the leader is a confident (at least confidently-acting) person with a bit of charisma, thus one who offers logical answers to questions from the group, and who may have the ability to demonstrate that they have good ideas. We often see this in groups that begin by discussing particular problems; if no one is specifically "in charge," the leader who emerges is often the person who demonstrates the most passion about the topic.

Or, they may simply be someone who is impatient for action, and goads others into a particular action that appears to achieve some common goals. In this case, the group tends to rally behind the "visionary." Sometimes, the visionary doesn't have much of a vision, but that doesn't mean they aren't capable of pursuing one (or of having one in the first place).

Another possibility is that one of this group recognizes that things can be done in a way to benefit everyone involved, much like the development of John Nash's gaming theory (the basis for the movie, "A Beautiful Mind"). The concern is not for the betterment, enrichment or even recognition of the leader, rather for the achievement of group goals, including the entire organization.

When we find this leader of the latter sort, John Collins, in his book Good to Great, calls them "Level 5" leaders. They are the ones who are passionate about achievement of the whole, not of themselves individually. These leaders aren't heralded, because they don't blow their own horns. They are too busy working toward meaningful goals to be distracted by something so counter-productive. Yet they do some particular things that we can see "proves" their leadership. Some of those things are where I'd like to focus this discussion.

Leaders who are passionate about their vision (they ALWAYS have a vision), are careful to make sure everyone in the organization knows what that vision is. They will indoctrinate everyone so that it is not simply a vision, but a tangible part of the environment, so much so that it will go home with employees at night. Everything that flows, then, is a reflection of that vision, because the vision becomes the beacon that guides the actions of everyone in the organization.

Those leaders know their people well: their personalities, their histories, their passions. The leader knows them because of the leadership involved in attracting and retaining the right people to "get the job done." They reach back to the theory of W. Edwards Deming, not necessarily for Statistical Process Control techniques (although they are valuable), but for Deming's "14 Points," one of which is to insure adequate and continuous training. If the right people are in the job and they are given the resources to get the job done, cheerleading is a waste of time, because these workers already get out of bed in the morning excited about going to work. Motivation? It's boiling inside each one of them, and they don't need slogans or mantras, or group meetings to cheer about history, because the "self-actualized" person is also self-motivated. They know their jobs, they know what's expected of them, and they know that they have a responsibility to the rest of the employees to do the best job they possibly can. One reason that happens is that the individual has been involved in development of their job and their responsibilities for that job, they've been informed about how their job fits into the overall scheme, and they are intimately involved in changes that occur in the company. Revolutionary? No, it's been in the books for decades.

When leaders develop this kind of employee and the managers to supervise those employees, they are freed up to do the visionary tasks: keeping the goal in sight, and making the course corrections necessary when changing conditions require them. Tweaking is a skill these leaders have that is taught in no school, which makes it that much more valuable.

There are some things we as individuals can do, if we want to develop our own leadership:

1. Keep focused on the primary goal for your company. Never let yourself be distracted from that.

2. Surround yourself not with those who only agree with you, but with the right people for the job you need done, then train them and provide them the tools to do the job.

3. Recognize the benefits of having different personalities around you. Not only do separate skill sets come with different personalities, but different approaches that are essential to your company's success.

4. Having hired the right people, get out of their way. If you must micromanage them, you don't need them. This is not a big problem, however, since they won't stay anyway, if you treat them with so little respect.

5. Remember always to consult your feedback loop in all your processes, to make sure things are working as you expect, and that you can make appropriate changes timely. Failure to do this with hasten the failure of your organization in total. Recall that your feedback loop is only as valuable as the people from whom you get feedback. Listen to them.

6. Know when you have exceeded your limitations, and acknowledge it. Then get help to overcome it.

Each of us has the capability to be a leader. We will only become effective leaders, however, when we lose our fear of making mistakes, and share responsibility for achievement of the goals of the organization. If those goals are our individual measures of achievement, then the organization will work to succeed and achieve; if they are not, we will be the transient leader that gets things going, but fails by failing to share credit and push for only the good of the organization.

Who Should Be a Leader?

Leadership is a topic that will typically interest businesses, managers, and CEOs. It is certainly very true that these are people who should try to understand what makes a good leader, and who can benefit from following leadership tips and advice.

In this section, we will be addressing the concept of leadership primarily from this angle. Most examples will pertain to leaders within organizations – whether those are charitable organizations, or whether they are massive corporations.

Leadership is a Life Skill

That said though, leadership is a life skill that should appeal to many more people than that!

That's because leadership is something that we are all called upon to provide at some point. One of the most common examples given is the parent-as-leader. If you are a parent, then you are required to provide guidance, tutelage, mentorship, and discipline for your children.

There will be times when you must inspire your children to be the greatest versions of themselves. But there will also be times when you need to provide strict and stern instructions that could save their lives!

And of course, there will be battles when trying to send them to bed!

An influential leader will know how to listen and make the child feel heard, while at the same time giving them the space and the protection they need to grow.

Leadership is a Superpower

Then there is the leader who emerges in a crisis. In this situation, leadership is a *superpower*.

Imagine that you're in a public space when suddenly the place collapses. You are trapped beneath the rubble and everyone is panicking, trampling one another. You need to work together in order to get help, and then to ration food and look after the injured.

In this situation, the person who rises to become the leader will be the person who is the most informed, and the person who is the most confident. If no one takes that mantle, then the situation could go south very quickly.

Being an influential leader is something that everyone should be capable of, so that they can rise to the occasion when it arises.

Leadership Outside of Work Environments

Finally, leadership is something that can make your social life and even your dating life that much more enjoyable. In every relationship and certainly every group dynamic, there is a power structure. Being the leader means being the one who gets to call the shots, who decides the activity, and who takes responsibility.

If you can be that person, then you'll find it does wonders for every aspect of your career.

So while leadership largely pertains to businesses, this is something we all should strive to cultivate. That's why throughout the book, we'll also be looking at how lessons and examples apply to those that are not working within an organizational hierarchy.

What Makes a Good Leader?

Leadership is incredibly valuable then, but unfortunately, it is not simple and easy. In fact, to demonstrate just how challenging leadership can be, keep in mind that a lot of people – including those who are in leadership roles – actually have no idea how to be a leader!

We have an image of what leadership means, and we often think of it as being "in charge." That means we need to micromanage our staff, and it means that if they do something wrong, we need to shout at them. Right?

This couldn't be further from what a good leader is.

Many leaders make the mistake here of thinking that they should act almost like a parent – where their team are the children. That means shouting when someone does something wrong, it means setting strict rules, and it means taking a "what I say goes" approach.

This is entirely the wrong attitude! When you approach your leadership role in this manner, you effectively smother the creativity and free thinking out of your team. That in turn means they are far less likely to do their best work. It also means they're very likely to spend a lot of their time feeling extremely stressed and not doing their best work. In fact, this could eventually leave to them quitting!

Many an office has slowly crumbled as a result of staff being literally driven out of their organizations.

Apart from anything else, it is not your place to shout at or reprimand your staff. You simply have no right to do so. If someone fails to hand work in on time, or if they are repeatedly late, and you then admonish them like a child in front of the entire team... what kind of message does this send?

Do you really think they are going to be at all likely to do their best work the next day?

And what about their colleagues and friends?

You are not their Mother or Father. They are free people who can act as they so wish. You don't have any real authority over them, and you certainly aren't superior to them.

Of course, if their behavior isn't congruent with what you need from your team, then you can politely end the agreement between you. But that is not the same as yelling at someone until they run out of the office crying. You are equals who have made an agreement and they have simply chosen to terminate the agreement. Understand this.

Likewise, don't make idle threats about their employment or their position. Some managers will literally tell their staff that they "have the power to fire them, you know." Again, do you really think this is going to encourage an optimum performance?

Don't you think they will end up just leaving the office entirely?

So how do you go about motivating a team that isn't working its best? We'll get to that more in future chapters, but the idea is to guide and not force. Your team were selected because they each should bring important new skills to the table. Your job is to create an environment where they feel comfortable to flex that muscle and employ those skills.

At the same time, you must inspire them to want to work, and to help place the right person on the right task so that they feel enthusiastic and excited to get to work. You need to provide clear and concise instructions, but then also step back and let your team's skills come to the forefront.

Being an influential leader is about nurturing, protecting, inspiring, guiding, and sacrificing. This guide will explain all that.

Communication Skills

One of the most important skills for any influential leader to cultivate, is communication. Your ability to write and speak will greatly impact on the way that people treat you, and the way that they respond to your instructions.

In the next chapter we'll talk about how to command respect, but this chapter is about simply putting across your point of view and your goals in a way that your colleagues understand.

How to Give Instructions Without Sounding Demanding

One of the most common ways that a leader will communicate is by giving instructions. In other words, you will provide either verbal or written steps and tips that can help someone to know what you need from them.

If you do this well, then you can ensure that everyone you speak with is providing the best possible work. But if you fail to provide concise and clear instructions, then you'll find that people end up doing the wrong kind of work – even when they mean well and have the best of intentions!

In future chapters, we're going to discuss the importance of allowing staff some element of control when choosing how they go about their work. While that's important, you will still of course have some factors that are not a matter of choice. You might have a specific deadline, you might have a particular budget, and there might be crucial points that need to be ticked off your list.

This is what you need to communicate in order for your team to operate as a well-oiled machine.

Consider these tips for providing clearer instructions:

- Provide all instructions right from the start. "Need to know basis" does not apply here.
- Don't assume anything. This is related to the above point. But if you have a strict

requirement, you cannot assume that your recipient will know that and plan their work around it. Don't wait until they've wasted hours doing something unnecessary to point out the precise specification!

- Be clear and concise. You can write a more detailed instruction if you want, but make sure that the key specifications are written in a bulleted list that is extremely simple to follow. A long paragraph runs the risk of being overlooked or ignored. People just want to get on with their work and "detailed" instructions are actually counterproductive!
- Demonstrate where possible. This is a very useful tip as it will help to show *exactly* what it is you're looking for. If you can't demonstrate, then finding a useful example or analogue of what you're looking for is also a good option. When asking a team to design a website for instance, it is a good idea to provide an example of the kind of thing you are looking for.
- Ask questions. If you ask questions then you will also be able to see if the person understands what you're saying. Likewise, give them the opportunity to ask questions if they have any.
- Make sure you have their full attention!

If you are in a crisis situation, or a parent, then providing a written checklist for your followers to read through is likely not an option!

In this case though, you can still list off a bulleted list of things that need to be done and your requirements. Again, it's about being concise and making sure it sticks in the mind:

"Call the police. Tell them that we're at X address. Then get back here as quickly as possible. Do you understand?"

Explain the Why

Another very big and important tip when providing instructions as a leader is to explain the "why." In other words, don't just tell your team what to do... tell them why they need to do it.

That means you should be explaining to your team why it is that what they are doing is important, and what the "end goal" is.

Instead of saying: do X, Y, and Z, you should say "We need to accomplish N, so do X, Y, and Z."

This does a few things. Firstly, it shows you trust the individual, and that trust can have a hugely positive impact on their willingness and enthusiasm. Likewise, knowing why what they are doing is important, can also provide a lot of additional motivation.

Secondly, it empowers the individual to think of their feet. If you provide clear instructions but the person doesn't understand the "why," then they won't be able to adapt if situations change. If they understand what needs to happen, then they can work around those problems to ensure that the outcome is still the one that you are looking for.

We'll see this idea come up time and again in this book: the idea that you must trust your team.

How to Command Respect and Speak So Others Will Listen

One of the most common questions in regards to leadership is this: should you be feared or liked?

Some leaders are effective because they frighten their team into submission. When you are a strict leader who has been known to reprimand the team, this can gain you a reputation for being no- nonsense. People therefore don't want to upset you, and thus they will do precisely what you instruct.

That's one approach anyway.

The other approach is to try and be liked. The idea here is that you become someone that people enjoy spending time with, and who can actually enjoy socializing as a part of the team. You are a friend to your team, which means that they will want to please you out of respect and out of kindness. Thus, when you ask them to do something, they do it!

So which is better?

Ultimately, neither. Your aim should be neither to terrify your staff into obedience – which simply creates ill feeling. Likewise, it shouldn't be to try and be the class clown, which will undermine respect.

Instead, be yourself. At the same time, be somewhat detached from the goings on of the office, such that you can take an impartial view when helping to settle disputes or help with personal issues.

Think of your role as "friendly guardian" or "kindly magician" more than "disciplinarian dictator" or "everyone's mate."

By doing this, you can command more respect by maintaining that slight air of separation, while at the same time giving your staff every reason to like you and no reason to think less of you.

The other reason to maintain a little more detached from the rest of the team is so that they can feel more relaxed and free to enjoy work. From that point, when you do step in, it will be more of a novelty to hear you getting involved. That in turn means that people will *listen* because it's so uncommon for you to speak in the first place!

From that point, it's all about the way you speak.

Speak So Others Will Listen

You've been in your office allowing your team to talk among themselves outside, checking in every now and then to ensure everyone is okay.

Now it is time to talk and to provide some strategy or direction. How do you do this so that people will listen and take what you have to say to heart?

Being able to speak in a commanding manner is actually one of the most important aspects of leadership outside of the office too.

If you want your children to pay attention to you, or if you want to rise to the occasion during a crisis, you need to know how to command attention.

Here are some of the most important tips.

Speak more slowly

Tip number one is to speak more slowly. Doing this will make you seem calmer, which in turn will make you seem more confident in what you have to say. At the same time, speaking more slowly makes your voice sound lower, and it makes you appear more intelligent. You'll also be less likely to stumble over your words this way.

Think of pretty much any heroic leader from fiction, and they will normally have a measured, deep, booming voice. You can accomplish this by simply speaking more slowly.

Leave Silence

Another tip is to recognize the power of silence. Don't be afraid to ask a rhetorical question and then let it hang. Don't be afraid to build some suspense for what you're about to say next!

Too many of us feel a constant urge to rush everything we have to say out at once. In fact though, it is often the silence between the individual statements that really has the most impact. It shows poise, control, patience, and confidence.

Speak With and To Emotion

Another extremely powerful tip, is to speak to and from emotion. What do we mean by this?

In sales, when trying to sell something, you are told to focus on the "value proposition." That means thinking about what it is that people gain from the product. Does your product make them happier? Healthier? Richer?

This will create an emotional hook, and emotion is what dictates behavior.

Well, attention is a type of behavior. And if you want people to listen, then you need to address something that seems pertinent to them – you need to appeal to their emotions. That means speaking about pride, about challenge, about success... it doesn't mean talking about numbers, or strategy.

Find the emotional hook and use this to elaborate and bring your point to life.

Likewise, you should try to channel that emotion yourself. How does this make you feel? Whether you're extremely happy, extremely confident, or something else... let that inform your choice of vocabulary.

Gesticulate

When you feel strongly about what you are saying, you will naturally gesticulate more and use bigger gestures. This unconscious signal makes us appear more congruent – it means our bodies and faces match our feelings.

That in turn means that people will be more engaged and more trusting in what we say. Look at anyone that you typically think of as charismatic, and you'll find that they all use these kinds of large gesticulations as they talk.

But Know When to be Still

When you aren't talking and getting your point across though, learn to be entirely still. This again will help you to evoke confidence and calm, which will create a powerful aura around you that makes other people want to listen.

As you continue to read this book, you'll see that many of these strategies go hand-in-hand with techniques that make a better leader. These body language and language tips are indicative and they correlate with the traits that you are trying to cultivate.

What is EQ?

Emotional intelligence refers to our ability to recognize and identify emotions in ourselves, and in others. That means being able to spot when someone is unhappy but also understanding why they might be unhappy. It means being able to prevent making someone angry, by empathizing with them and understanding how best to handle their current situation.

Emotional intelligence can make a drastic difference to your success in a leadership role, and to the happiness and productivity of the team.

Imagine that you've spent all day working on something, and you're extremely proud of what you have accomplished. You submit the work and then you get the following response:

"Please fix the error on page 3." Or worse:

"Thank you for this work. A good effort overall, but this does NOT conform to the style guidelines set out in the last meeting. Were you even listening?

In addition, there are three mistakes right toward the

end. Please do be careful to pay attention when working as it creates more work for everyone else when you don't."

Oh and for added good measure, these responses were placed in a public forum where everyone could see the feedback.

So, what is wrong with these responses? Clearly you made mistakes, and you're just being called out on them! Moreover, the manager/colleague has used polite language (please and thank you). They even said "good effort."

Of course, that's not how you're going to react to someone critiquing work that you spent time and effort on however. And that approach is hardly going to make you want to quickly fix the problem.

A far better approach, would be to start by acknowledging the hard work, and saying something positive about the final product. This acknowledgement immediately wins the favour of the person receiving the feedback, and shows them that you value the effort they've already put in.

You might then follow this up with a complement or two. This can help to balance out the negative feedback, again so as to keep morale high and to demonstrate that you do respect their work and effort. You can then include the negative feedback in a subtle way – while being sure to show understanding for what led to the issues – before following it up with something more positive. This is often referred to as the "sandwich" approach to giving feedback. For obvious reasons!

This now leaves that person far more likely to make the change, all without feeling insulted or overlooked by their management. Add to this a knowledge of the person you are speaking to and what helps them to work their best, and you can respond in a way that will be motivating, encouraging, but practical.

There are countless interactions every day that will require this kind of sensitivity.

Consider that top response too. This is seemingly innocuous but a simple fix could make all the difference (leaving aside for a moment the failure to acknowledge all the hard work):

"Please could you fix the error on page 3?"

The only change here is that the "please" has been moved to the front of the sentence. But while that might seem small, it creates a hugely different impression. Placing the "please" up front shows the reader that you are genuinely asking them to do something and you are grateful.

But when the start of the sentence is "fix this" it sounds like an absolute command. The "please" now becomes an afterthought that just so happens to be there.

If you are trying to get someone to do something and that person isn't strictly someone that you have authority over, then this will become even more frustrating for them. Now it looks like you think you can boss them around. It comes across as curt, arrogant, and presumptuous.

Again, it might not seem like a big deal, but moving one word a few places can make a huge difference.

Now imagine countless interactions with hundreds of people in a single day, and hopefully you can recognize the crucial role of emotional intelligence.

Models and Measures

The skills of emotional intelligence may be acquired throughout life. You are able to boost your own "EQ" by learning how to speedily reduce stress, connect to your emotions, communicate nonverbally, utilize humor and play to deal with challenges, and defuse conflicts with confidence and self- assurance.

Numerous measures of emotional intelligence utilized in scientific research, especially those sold for utilization in industrial and organizational settings, are not based on any of the aforementioned theories of emotional intelligence.

2 of these measures: the Levels of Emotional Awareness Scale (LEAS) and the Self- Report Emotional Intelligence Test (SREIT)

1) The LEAS

The Levels of Emotional Awareness Scale is a self-report measure of emotional intelligence specified to assess the extent to which individuals are aware of emotions in both themselves and other people.

The measure is based on a hierarchical theory of emotional intelligence, more specifically of emotional cognizance, which consists of 5 sub-levels: physical sensations, action inclinations, single emotions, blends of emotion, and blends of these blends of emotional experience. The Levels of Emotional Awareness Scale consists of twenty scenarios involving 2 individuals and an emotion-eliciting position.

The participant must indicate how they'd feel in the situation and how the other individual in the scenario would feel in the situation. Each scenario gets a score from 0-5 . The participant gets a score for self (awareness of emotions in oneself), for other (awareness of emotion in other people), and a total emotional awareness score (a mean of self and other).

The Levels of Emotional Awareness Scale was determined to be related to two subscales of emotional intelligence: perceiving emotions in stories and estimating feelings of characters in struggle. An independent review concluded that it's only if minimally related to emotional intelligence and would more precisely be classified as a measure of processing style instead of ability.

2) The SREIT

The Self Report Emotional Intelligence Test is a thirty-three item self- report measure of emotional intelligence. Initially based on early writings on emotional intelligence by Mayer and Salovey, this test has been picked apart for not properly mapping onto the Salovey and Mayer model of E.I. and thus measuring another concept of emotional intelligence.

Participants are asked to signal their reactions to items reflecting adaptive tendencies towards emotional intelligence according to a 5-point scale, with "1" representing firm agreement and "5" representing firm disagreement.

As mentioned, independent reviewers found a lack of content validness. However, the authors report content validity as being passable, with the thirty-three items.

Success and EI

Research on the predictive implication of E.I. over I.Q. was spurred by an initial publication on the subject which claimed that emotional intelligence may be "as potent, and at times more potent, than I.Q.

Much of this claim was founded on preceding research revealing that the predictive nature of I.Q. on job performance wasn't promising, with I.Q. Reporting from 10-25% of the variance in job performance.

The results of longitudinal fields of study further implicated emotional intelligence as being significant. One field of study involving 450 boys reported that I.Q.

had little relation to work and personal success; rather, more crucial in determining their success was their power to handle frustration, control emotions, and get along with other people. Although this field of study didn't attend to emotional intelligence straight off, the elements which it handled (the power to regulate one's emotions and comprehend the emotions of other people) are a few of the central tenants of the emotional intelligence concept.

Although research exists supporting the argument that emotional intelligence does lend to individual cognitive-based performance over and above the level ascribed to general intelligence , present theories tend to be more sensible regarding the incremental benefits of E.Q. over I.Q. Studies emphasize that emotional intelligence by itself is likely not a strong forecaster of job performance. Rather, it supplies a foundation for emotional competencies which are strong predictors of job performance.

Later works, attempt to theoretically clear up the relationship between I.Q. and E.Q., and their respective pertinence to job performance. I.Q. plays a sorting function, determining the sorts of jobs people are capable of holding. I.Q. is a solid predictor of what jobs people may enter as well as a solid forecaster of success among the general population in general. For instance, in order to become a physician, an person needs an above average

I.Q. Emotional intelligence, on the other hand, is described as a solid predictor of who will excel in a specific line of work when levels of I.Q. are comparatively equivalent.

When the people are being compared to a narrow pool of individuals in a specific line of work in a particular organization, specifically in the higher levels, the predictive power of I.Q. for outstanding performance among them de-escalates greatly. In that circumstance, E.Q. would be the stronger forecaster of people who outperform other people.

Thus, the physicians in a specific clinic would all have similarly above average I.Q.'s. What would distinguish the most successful physicians from the others would be their levels of emotional intelligence.

The Crucial Importance of Emotional Intelligence

We've discussed a few examples of bad leadership in this book so far, and unfortunately these examples are not uncommon.

There are a huge number of very bad leaders out there, and in fact it's seemingly quite rare these days to find someone who is happy with their management!

Why is this?

A big part of the problem, is that many organizations don't look at leadership as a quality that needs to be trained, or even that is innate. They don't see leadership as a quality at all in fact – rather just a position!

This perspective is apparent in hiring and promotion activities. An organization might have a team of data analysts, ad managers, sales representatives, and accountants. They've all been working there for years beneath a successful manager.

Then one day, that manager leaves, and thus a power vacuum is created. Either that, or the organization offers the manager some meaningless promotion…

Whatever the case, the company now needs a new manager, and so what they will end up doing is looking at their existing staff and then finding a member who they think deserves the position – that will be someone who has been working there for a long time, or who has been doing a good job. Let's say data analyst Jeff.

But data analyst Jeff is not a leader, and now suddenly he is in charge of 20 people. He has neither *learned* the skills necessary to be a leader, nor been blessed with them naturally.

He lacks emotional intelligence.

This also tends to happen when someone is put in an unknowing leadership role. For example, let's say you have a team of writers on a magazine, and suddenly a new copy checker is brought in. Their job is to make sure there are no mistakes, and when they find one, they need to hand it back to the member of the team so that they can fix it (not a great set-up, but it works in this situation).

That copy checker is not just fulfilling a role, but they're also calling out team members, and they're giving them work. In other words, they are leaders – even though it might not immediately be apparent that this is the nature of their job. Again, this means that they are more likely to lack the inherent leadership skills that they really need in order to be successful.

5 Ways to Improve Your Social Skills and Increase Your Emotional Intelligence

The term "social skills" is incredibly broad, but it is also used correctly in the context of emotional intelligence. When it comes to emotional intelligence, your social skills refers to how you handle and influence other's emotions effectively. Emotional intelligence starts with your understanding of your feelings and being able to effectively manage them to achieve your goals. When you can understand and manage yourself, you can begin to learn how to understand the feelings of others and how to influence them. Here are five ways that you can improve your social skills to increase your emotional intelligence.

Work on Your Communication Skills

Your communication skills are a vital part of having good emotional intelligence. People who demonstrate high emotional intelligence can effectively listen to others and convey their own thoughts and feelings appropriately. Good communicators listen well to others and make sure that they understand what is being said. This allows them to register and act upon the emotional cues so that they can respond appropriately.

Improve Your Conflict Management Skills

Conflicts and disagreements are a natural part of life and can happen at any time. The art of managing and resolving disputes is a crucial aspect of emotional intelligence and is critical for your success both personally and professionally. Improving your conflict management skills starts by being aware of the importance of diplomacy and tact, and how they can be used to diffuse a situation.

Improve Your Leadership Skills

Your leadership skills are inextricably linked to emotional intelligence. Leaders must be tuned into their own and other's emotions if they want to be influential. Good leaders tend to have high emotional intelligence because they can articulate a vision and provide support and guidance to their colleagues while holding them accountable for their actions.

Develop Persuasion and Influencing Skills

Persuasion is the art of motivating others and winning them over to your ideas. People who have high emotional intelligence are apt at persuading others to their proposed course of action. They can read the emotional currents of any given situation and fine-tune their response to appeal to everyone involved.

Work on Building Rapport

If you want to improve your emotional intelligence, then it is vital that you figure out how to build and maintain relationships with others. Developing this skill will lead you to have better relationships and an increased ability to get on with life. Not only are highly emotionally intelligent people good at building rapport, but they also work to maintain the relationships they already have.

When you have high emotional intelligence, it's obvious based on your social skills. If you want to improve your emotional intelligence, then you need to work on these five ways for developing your social skills.

Tools

Ultimately, the best improvements in emotional intelligence will come from life experience and knowing yourself.

Life experience is important because it teaches you sensitivity, and it teaches you never to assume what is going on in someone's life.

Consider for a minute that someone comes into work looking scruffy and untidy, so you tell them that it isn't good enough and they need to do better if they want to keep working with you. They promptly burst into tears.

Why? Turns out a parent died last night, and the only reason they still came into work was because they were so behind and they're so conscientious.

You can never know what is going on in someone's life, which is why you should always give them the benefit of the doubt. By having richer life experiences, you can experience this reality first hand, and gain a better understanding of what someone might be going through. Spending time with a wider range and variety of people can also help a great deal.

Listen with open ears, don't jump to conclusions, and give people space to explain what is going on with them.

But this kind of life experience and understanding takes a long time to cultivate. That's why you should also focus on learning to know your own thoughts and feelings better. By understanding what makes you tick, you'll be better able to understand and help manage the emotions of others.

One way to do this is by practicing CBT and mindfulness. That means spending time reflecting on your own thoughts and motivations, and being more consciously aware of where your attention is, what you're thinking about, and how you're feeling.

Managing your own emotions is also an important aspect of leadership so that is a great added bonus, as we will discuss in a later chapter.

For Parents

This is one of the tips in this book with the most obvious payoffs for parents. When trying to help your children to learn and grow, understanding their emotions is absolutely key. In particular, it is critical that you understand the importance of letting them feel "heard."

When a child is very upset or angry, a parent can often attempt to try and "calm them down" by telling them not to be. This unfortunately will not usually help, as it basically tells them not to feel the way they are feeling – which often just makes them more angry and upset!

Instead, show first that you understand their emotions: say "that must have made you really angry, right?" or "I understand why you're upset."

In a Crisis

In a crisis, your job is to keep the mood of everyone in the situation calm. You are now managing the emotions of everyone present, to try and ensure the very best outcomes.

This means making sure that you stay calm yourself, and that you instruct clearly and recognize the role that panic and stress can play in the efficiency with which tasks get carried out.

Why It's Important to Know Your Team

As a leader, your job is to achieve some kind of goal, or reach some kind of target, all by encouraging your team to do their best work. Again, it is not your job to micromanage that team or to do the work for them. Rather, you are simply encouraging them and giving them a safe place to exercise their inherent abilities.

Be Genuinely Interested in Knowing Your Team

One of the most important aspects of getting the most out of a team is to know them well. That means taking a personal interest in them as people, as well as having a solid understanding of what it is they do for your organization and how they work best.

This then allows you to anticipate how a team member is likely to react, and it allows you to put them in the best place at the best time, to put them on the most appropriate projects, and to generally help them to perform at their best level.

One of the most fundamental aspects of this, is to recognize what the key skills of each member of your team are, and then how you can put them to the best use. If you have a member of your team and you're failing to maximize their potential, then you are simply *wasting money*.

Let's consider an example. Imagine for a moment that you run a website on a complex topic such as programming. You have hired some technical writers and you're paying them a lot in order to write in-depth tutorials and articles, and to stay up-to-date with the latest information.

But you also have those same writers uploading their own articles to the site. And you're incredibly strict about formatting. You want them to make sure that they use the right fonts, that they are using the right sizes for images, and that they add the right meta tags.

To make things more complicated, your formatting guidelines change every few weeks. You then have the writers jump back into their work in order to add those updated changes.

And when they miss some formatting? Then all heck breaks loose and you yell at them until they change their ways.

That sounds rather destructive right? But it's how a lot of teams will handle this kind of situation. In fact, this example is taken from a real-life experience.

The worst thing is that this means the programmer is now being paid a LOT of money in order to do work that anyone could do for a fraction of the price. Why have a top writer spend all day changing image sizes?

Instead, you could hire someone for a tiny amount of the price, and you could then use your best talent to generate the meaningful work. You'd double your output, keep everyone happier, and end up with a much better end result.

What's more, is that your staff will soon become miserable if they are spending all of their time doing work that doesn't engage, challenge, or reward them in any way. And we'll explore more about why this matters in a moment.

Putting Your Team Together

Another important reason to know your team well, is so that you can know who works best with who, and then make sure that they are paired according to that information.

This is more complex than simply putting people together if they get on! That's because people who get on can often end up actually distracting one-another, meaning it might even make more sense to pair people together who challenge and improve each other.

Think as well about when to mix up your team, or how staying together could ultimately hurt performance. We've all heard how Steve Jobs introduced open plan offices to Pixar in order to encourage chance encounters between animators, script writers, actors, and the rest of the team.

Likewise, consider factors like "convergence and divergence." This tells us how people placed in groups will typically grow more alike over time, while also becoming more different from those around them. This process can result in a "tribe-like" attitude, which might ultimately create problems within the office.

Getting the Most Out of Your Team

Finding ways to get the most out of staff is a constant struggle for business owners and managers who are constantly told different things and given different information. One minute it's a good idea to incentivise staff with potential bonuses, perks and rewards, the next that same advice is apparently wrong. How do you know what to believe and what do you do for best? And why is there so much disagreement in the first place?

Motivating Your Team

Well as it happens, the question really comes down to how you define motivation. There is of course more than one type of motivation and as the needs of the organization vary, so the best ways to get more out of staff change too. It turns out that when you're trying to encourage creativity and out-of-the-box thinking specifically, then incentives are more damaging than helpful.

And to understand why this is the case we need to break things down further and examine exactly what we mean by creativity. How do you define creativity? How do you measure problem solving ability?

While opinions vary on this matter, one aspect that is generally agreed to be indicative of wider creativity and problem-solving skill is what's known as 'functional fixedness'. This term refers to the ability or inability that we have to think of objects in ways other than their intended use. So if you were to take a hammer for instance, functional fixedness would be the 'cognitive bias' that prevented you from thinking of using it to scratch your back. It's a hammer, not a back scratcher.

A great demonstration of this flaw in our thinking is something called 'the candle box experiment'. Here participants are given a box of tacks and a candle and they're asked to attach the candle to the wall in such a way that it can burn while being poised there. Most people will try to tack the candle to the wall which will of course meet with disaster, but after a while they will start to think of alternative solutions at which point they get over their functional fixedness, realize that the box itself is a useful resource, and then tack that to the wall to stand the candle in.

The reason this is relevant to this particular discussion is that incentives and external motivation have actually been shown to make participants slower to come up with the solution.

The reason for this is that motivation can actually create some stress as you feel the need to amp yourself up to work towards the reward. This in turn can result in a kind of 'tunnel vision' as you approach your work – focussed hard on the task at hand.

Conversely creativity it appears is most likely to occur when we step back and relax. This in turn helps us to allow our minds to wander and enables us to see more connections between disparate ideas. And many believe that this is what creativity really is: the ability to combine unconnected ideas and combine them in unique new ways. Other studies show that a sense of ownership and pride in their work can also help to encourage staff to be more creative and original with their thinking, while allowing discourse between team members has been shown to incubate the generation of new ideas too.

So if you want your staff to provide data entry then you can help them to do this by providing incentives and rewards. Because this kind of role does not require creativity, that will be a suitable method! For other more creative tasks however it may be better to help them to relax, to let them take a step back and to provide a safe space to work their very best.

Protection

If stress can dampen creativity and prevent your team from producing their best work, the logical alternative is to reduce stress for your team as much as you possibly can.

That in turn means you need to take the flack. And that's a huge part of what it really means to be a leader. What being a leader really means, is taking responsibility.

The bad leader will shout at their staff when things are going badly and blame them – failure to take responsibility.

This is despite the fact that the bad leader will micromanage every tiny decision and leave the team with no freedom of their own.

But the good leader will let the team work in the way they do best, and will then take the flack from upper management when things don't go to plan. Why? Because when your staff feel as though they are protected and safe, that's when they are able to do their best work. We've already seen how this can improve creative problem solving... but of course it also helps to improve work satisfaction, and to generally ensure that your team are happy working away.

Being a leader ultimately means taking the hit, and being willing to sacrifice your own sanity for theirs!

For Parents

Parents can benefit the most of all from this tip. One of the most important things to do as a parent, is to provide a source of unconditional love, as well as physical safety.

By meeting your child's most basic needs like this, you give them the confidence they need to explore, learn, and make their own mistakes. A child who receives nothing but love and encouragement will have the confidence to venture out, to try new things, and to express themselves. This will ultimately lead to a far more even development that makes them into fully functioning adults some day!

In many ways, you can consider the role of a manager as something similar. You provide the "unconditional love" by creating a warm, team environment that protects the staff from the outside harsh realities of your organization.

Is It Better To Be Feared Or Liked?

If you were to stop reading here and just work with all the information we've covered so far, you would now be a leader who was inspiring, courageous and well equipped to motivate their team. You can even help to weather a storm and keep your team motivated and calm when things That's a great start but there's a lot more to it than that.

For example, there is the small matter of knowing how you are going to control your team. Because so far we've kind of dealt with an ideal scenario where everyone believes in your vision and you are all working toward the same goal. Like the Queen song...

But what happens when some people really don't want to be there? What happens when two people think it's all just a joke?

What happens when someone has a bad attitude and is just trying to create problems for everyone?

This is when leaders can be split into two groups.

You have the one group that will plead with their staff and attempt to be 'liked'. They might make it into a joke, try to be on the 'same page' against the system, or to generally chummy up.

Then you have the other type of leader that will instill fear and tell the member of staff that they will be fired or sent to another department if they continue.

Machiavelli asked whether it is better to be 'feared or loved'. So which is it?

Well, Machiavelli himself actually said it is better to be feared. But that was in a very different time and place.

Suffice to say that it is not good to want to be best mates with your staff. This is perfectly demonstrated by the character of David Brent from The Office who is more interested in trying to be funny rather than being in charge. Unfortunately, there does need to be some distance between a leader and their team and it's important that you maintain a little respect. Once your team has seen you drunk and curled round a toilet at the office Christmas party, it will impact negatively on your ability to instruct them on what to do.

Likewise though, taking a fully 'fear based' approach is also a mistake. This ultimately makes you into the enemy and it creates a stressful work environment for your team. It also prevents your team from attempting to be fully creative or expressing themselves because they will be fearful of repercussions.

So we need to reframe the question. Is it better to be feared or liked? Neither – it's better to be respected. You need to be calm and in charge in such a way that people want you to like them. That will be a) because they respect you and b) because they understand that you can help them and that you want what is best for the team. If your team sees what you do for them, knows you believe in what you are doing and respects your ability and your capabilities, then they should respect you. If you present yourself as capable, calm and cool, then they should want your respect as well.

And guess what? One of the very best ways to gain respect is to show someone else respect. The best way to be liked is to be nice to someone – to be likeable. The best way to be respected is to be respectful so that there is a mutual understanding.

A good leader needs to be able to work with colleagues from all walks of life and should value what each of them brings to the team equally. In fact, more diverse voices will mean a more diverse set of opinions and views and more diverse skill set!

And so you can occasionally make jokes at your own expense, join in with the fun and even allow others to point fun at you – this shows confidence and strength. The key is to make sure you don't allow this to cross a line and that you don't tolerate staff trying to push their luck by taking a joke too far, seeing how far you will go or being disrespectful. Likewise, you mustn't allow them to test the limits of what they can get away with and this is especially important because it can be unfair on their team and also set a bad precedent. Once one person realizes they can clock off early or stretch their cigarette break to 20 minutes, so can everyone else.

But of course you can't just punch someone who is causing trouble in your team. So what can you do? How can you ultimately demonstrate your authority and get someone to sit down and get on with their work? If your attempts to motivate and to demonstrate the reasons behind your requests aren't working, then what can you do to deal with dissidents?

Dealing With Dissidents

Of course there is more than one kind of disruption in any team and there is more than one type of problematic member. So the way you deal with insubordination is going to depend on the scenario.

We have some options: these will start with the first and most desirable options you have available to you and end with the final and most regretful options.

Transformismo

The first option is to welcome the challenge. If someone is not happy with your leadership or the direction you're taking the team, then you could view this as a valid concern. They clearly must have some motivation for not liking the way things are going and that is useful information to you. They have a divergent opinion so instead of staying glued to your confirmation balance – listen to what they have to say and invite them to suggest an alternative option. Often this will take someone so much by surprise that it can earn you instant success.

Better yet, take someone who is trying to encourage more people to side against you and put them in a position of power and responsibility. This is a technique called 'transformismo' that was championed by Italian ruler Mussolini. It's the perfect solution because it a) demonstrates to that person the difficulty of being in your position and shows them that leadership is not so easy as they might like to make out and b) busies them to the point where they can't become problematic.

Or as Sun Tsu put it: keep your enemies close...

Explain and Use Social Influence

Another thing to do is to explain to the person who is behaving inappropriately the damage that they are doing not only to the organization but also themselves and the team. This is once again the power of 'why'.

If someone is going out for longer cigarette breaks for example, then you should simply explain to them that in doing that, they are forcing their colleagues to pick up their slack. If they value their friendship with those colleagues, then they will not like the thought of this and might reconsider their actions. Likewise, you can explain that it has been noted and that when it comes time for a review, it might hold them back for a promotion.

And again, invite them to make a suggestion. Ask them why they feel the need to spend outside. Ask them what it is they want from this interaction and see if you can come up with an alternative solution. If they feel they can't stand being in the office, then perhaps you need to change the layout of the office? Again, this is a highly effective method as if they feel they're being listened to, then they might feel obligated to give a little as well. Better yet, you might be able to successfully remove the problem altogether.

Of course the temptation here is to make an example of that person and to tell the rest of the team how they're not pulling their weight. This is a mistake because it will a) make that person feel victimized and b) create disharmony in your ranks that will ultimately be bad for business. What you can do though is to praise those who are putting in more hours and make sure that they know that you're aware in the difference between their efforts and those of their lackadaisical colleagues.

Carrying Out Punishment

One thing you must never do is to shout, get angry or get upset. If you rant and rave at your subordinate, then it will make you appear despotic and it will make the person you are shouting at feel victimized. This can result in people eventually feeling the need to 'stand up to you' and could potentially result in a full scale mutiny.

Moreover, what you're doing here is to completely misunderstand the terms of the agreement between you and your team members (this is a little different for parents).

Ultimately, when you are in charge of someone in a work setting, it only means that they agreed to work for your organization. It doesn't mean you have supreme authority of them and you certainly don't have the right to reprimand them as a child. You might be their 'superior' in terms of work hierarchy but you are equal in reality. So what is really going on here is an agreement – the agreement is that they will do what you ask (within reason) in exchange of payment and workplace satisfaction.

If that agreement doesn't work out, then either of you has the right to terminate it at any time. But you do not have the right to make them feel small.

This is why it's highly important not to make this permanent and not to make it look as though you have lost your cool. Instead, just keep things polite and civil but carry out what you have to do. And the easiest way to do that? That would be to have a clear set of rules and repercussions for not following those rules. For instance: people caught not working their full set of hours will be required to make up those hours in the evenings and weekends.

With a clearly defined set of actions and outcomes, you can carry out what needs to be done in a cool and collected fashion without making it personal and without it ever seeming 'unfair'. It's the same rule for everyone, they had prior warning and you are simply following a predefined set of instructions.

This is one more reason not to become 'too' chummy with your team though – it can make it hard when you do have to take this kind of action and it can lead to accusations of favoritism or personal feelings getting in the way.

Understanding Characters And Choosing The Right person for the job

Perhaps the most important part of creating a working team is to understand the importance of different characters and what they can each bring to your organization.

This means firstly respecting and understanding all the different skills that your different employees can offer (or your family!). A big part of leadership is delegating and that means you need to know each member of your team well enough to know who is best suited to which job. You can get a workload completed twice as efficiently, simply by giving the right jobs to the right people!

This also means respecting and acknowledging that your team will be better experienced and better equipped than you in some areas. This is important because it is another way you will show respect and give them more autonomy. BUT you should have enough understanding of each of their roles to understand what they're doing and to help offer direction. A good leader in an IT firm should know a little about SEO, a little about coding and a little about marketing so that they can help each member work together.

What's also important though is to understand the differences in personalities, which can also help you to better understand the strengths and weaknesses of each team member and help you to better relate to problems they might be having.

Some psychometric tests will define people in a business as falling into one of the four main 'types':

- Dominant

- Expressive

- Introverted

- Relational

The dominant type of course is the 'type A' personality who is loud, driven and high achieving. They might make a good leader someday but they will also undoubtedly rub people up the wrong way until they get some experience under their belt.

The expressive type is the great communicator who is the natural sales person and should thus be given those types of tasks.

Introverts are self-motivated and work well on their own but they may be shy (not always) and would probably not be the right people to give presentations or sales tasks to. Conversely, they might be quite creative and useful in those scenarios.

Finally, you have the relational type who is driven by their outward relations and who is a great peace maker and communicator. These people can provide the glue in a team and help to prevent arguments.

What is the best type of personality for your team?

All of them! And if you are going to be making a small splinter cell to send to a tradeshow or to work on a particular project, you'll want to try and include one of each type of person in order to get the most from them all. That way you'll have a lot of different influences, ultimately resulting in the best final outcome.

Of course you can go much deeper than that too with tests like the Myers-Briggs Personality Type Test – but this is a very lengthy and in- depth measure and very time consuming. Ultimately no psychometric test will offer a perfect or complete picture of a person's personality but the key is simply to know your team as well as is possible and to understand how they work with other members of the team and where you can put them to get the most out of them.

The Power of Ownership

At this point, you have a team that is happy to work and that feels safe and protected doing so. But we still haven't honed in on precisely how you motivate them to actually get down to it.

Give Others Freedom To Work On What They Want

The answer to that little puzzle then, is to give your team ownership over the work that they do. That means to let your team make decisions about how they're going to work, what they're going to focus on, and even what it might end up looking like. You can even let them create their own projects.

This means giving them the freedom to experiment and a sense of ownership. There's a reason that Google give their staff free time to work on their own projects... and happen to be one of the largest and most transformative businesses in the world!

When you do this, you make someone innately and inherently invested in the project, and you ensure that they love what they are doing.

Don't Force Someone To Do What They Don't Enjoy

Here's the stark reality: you can't really force someone to do what they don't enjoy to the best of their ability. If you force someone to work on a project they find dull, then of course they will work on that project. But they won't give it their all, and much of the work will be sub-par.

Conversely, if you get someone to work on their passion project and this project has their name on it, suddenly they become far more invested and they actually want to go to work. They'll work harder at the project because it has their name on it, and because it makes them feel alive. This could improve their career, and it's something they can be proud of at the end of the day.

When you micromanage someone and control every small decision that someone makes, they are given zero control or ownership over that thing. This in turn means that they won't be at all invested or interested in it.

Likewise, if you refuse to listen to their point of view, or if you know they have big problems with the way that the work is being approached, again you shouldn't be surprised if they lack motivation and don't do their best work.

This is why the job of the leader is to take on a lot of responsibility for what happen to protect their team, while at the same time giving the team more creative control. That's why it takes a lot of bravery to be a true leader.

This is another reason it is so important to explain to people why they should do something.

In a Crisis

In a crisis this same approach applies. That's because you will likely be yelling out roles for people: asking someone to call for help, while another person stops the bleeding for example.

Again, you can't be everywhere and do everything. Your job is to give the instructions to the person attempting to do the job, and then to let them make the key decisions about how to do it.

For Parents

This is another tip that is very important and useful for parents! Young children always want to feel involved and they want to feel ownership over what they're doing.

Try and feed your child their vegetables and they will often refuse. You might take this as a sign that they don't want those vegetables. So what do you do? Promise them sweets if they eat their vegetables? (Remember: rewards can actually harm productivity!)

Or do you fight them to try and get them to eat?

The solution often is to let them hold the spoon, or to let them choose which vegetables they want. You're still guiding their behavior, but by letting them learn and feel involved, they will be much happier to acquiesce.

How To Deal With Difficult Decisions

Sometimes being a leader means making the hard call. In fact, this is very often what it means. Remember, the job of the captain is to go down with the ship. You are trying to protect your team so that they feel confident to do their best work. And that sometimes means taking a serious hit.

Here is how to deal with things when the going gets rough.

How To Stay Calm As a Leader

What do you do when you lose your biggest client and you think that your company is going to no longer be able to afford to employ everyone? What do you do when your family is in debt and you need to tell them that you have to downsize your home?

The single and most important job as a leader is to remain calm. Remember: you are protecting your team and taking the hits so that they can do their best work in a safe environment. That extends to remaining calm in a crisis so that they don't have to panic.

If your team is worrying about lay-offs, then how are they supposed to focus and do their best work? This can ultimately become a self-fulfilling prophecy if allowed to escalate.

Consider that your team will look to you to set the tone. If you seem panicked, then they will panic. If you seem calm, then they will see that you have it under control.

Not only that, but you'll also be able to appear more confident in your leadership, and ultimately it is only by being confident in yourself that you can inspire confidence in others!

This is not the same as hiding the truth from your team. One of the worst things you can do for a team from a communication standpoint is to lie and tell them everything is okay when it really isn't. While this might seem as though it would further the cause of helping your team to stay focussed on their work, the truth is that it will eventually come out in the wash. This means you'll then lose the trust of your team, and that they won't know how best to prepare themselves for the coming event. Be truthful, reassuring, transparent, and calm.

How to Handle Difficult Team Members

Another issue that you will find yourself struggling with is the occasional mutinous individual. Whether you are the captain of a ship, or you are a team leader on the meat aisle, you will find there are always people who don't want to do as you say.

So what do you do in this situation?

As before, you are not to reprimand, threaten, or punish the individual. Once more, this is not only morally a dubious position to take – it is also simply a bad strategy! This is because, isolating, alienating, and aggravating someone who already intends on disrupting your leadership is a bad idea. Doing this will only cause that person to recruit more of your team to their cause, and to spend their time thinking about how wrong your style of leadership is!

Ever heard the saying "keep your friends close, and your enemies closer"? This is a saying that Italian autocrat Mussolini believed in strongly, which is why he coined the phrase "Transformismo" to describe the way he would deal with dissidents. This basically meant giving that vocal opponent a position of authority within his organization.

This strategy can often work wonders, as it turns that critic into someone who is now working with you to improve your leadership. They can see first-hand the challenges you face, and that perhaps life isn't quite as simple as they believed it to be. Not only that, but it ensures they feel valued and cherished by the organization, rather than ostracised.

AND it lets you keep a close eye on them...

Challenges for Modern Leaders

Being a leader today is different than it ever has been before, and this is particularly true within organizations.

If you are a leader within an organization, then there is a high chance that you will find yourself dealing with a range of new situations and tools that alter the way that you lead.

For instance, you might today need to lead from afar. That means in other words, that you are going to be using collaboration tools to work with distributed teams all around the world. This can make life much more difficult, as you won't be able to know precisely what your staff are doing, or whether they're really carrying out the work you set them!

Likewise, parents now need to deal with new challenges – which include such things as mobile phones and the internet. Again, this prevents them from knowing everything that is going on in their children's lives, making it harder than ever for them to protect them and guide them.

There are several ways that we can react to these changes. One of the most common, is to try and reign in our followers even more – to place even stricter and more controlling rules and restrictions on them. The hope is that we can this way get a better idea of what they are doing and thus control their actions.

But the truth is that doing this actually often has the opposite effect. Again, the most powerful way to motivate someone who is miles away from you, is to make sure that the tasks you give them are inherently motivating. That is to say they should be rewarding in their own right – because they offer a sense of ownership to the person completing them, and a sense of being highly involved.

If you notice that someone is falling behind, don't assume it is because they are lazy! Instead, ask why they aren't motivated enough to complete the work you have set them?

Likewise, many parents understand that telling their children they can't drink alcohol will often force them to act out and drink even more without telling their parents! Giving them that bit of freedom – allowing them to have some drinks in a controlled and safe environment – can often help to avoid them feeling the need to completely rebel.

And so it is with the internet: try and block or restrict your child's internet access and they will only find a way around it. But give them that access and tell them that you are doing so because you trust them, and you might find they are less likely to betray that trust.

Your job as a leader is to protect, to inspire, and to guide. It is NOT to control. This is true even when you are dealing with the modern, complex challenges of leadership. In fact, that only makes this approach even more vital.

Awaken The Leader In You: 10 Easy Steps To Developing Your Leadership Skills

"The miracle power that elevates the few is to be found in their industry, application, and perseverance, under the promptings of a brave determined spirit." - Mark Twain

Many motivational experts like to say that leaders are made, not born. I would argue the exact opposite. I believe we are all natural born leaders, but have been deprogrammed along the way. As children, we were natural leaders - curious and humble, always hungry and thirsty for knowledge, with an incredibly vivid imagination; we knew exactly what we wanted, were persistent and determined in getting what we wanted, and had the ability to motivate, inspire, and influence everyone around us to help us in accomplishing our mission. So why is this so difficult to do as adults? What happened?

As children, over time, we got used to hearing, No, Don't, and Can't. No! Don't do this. Don't do that. You can't do this. You can't do that. No! Many of our parents told us to keep quiet and not disturb the adults by asking silly questions. This pattern continued into high school with our teachers telling us what we could do and couldn't do and what was possible. Then many of us got hit with the big one institutionalized formal education known as college or university. Unfortunately, the traditional educational system doesn't teach students how to become leaders; it teaches students how to become polite order takers for the corporate world. Instead of learning to become creative, independent, self-reliant, and think for themselves, most people learn how to obey and intelligently follow rules to keep the corporate machine humming.

Developing the Leader in you to live your highest life, then, requires a process of unlearning by self-remembering and self-honoring. Being an effective leader again will require you to be brave and unlock the door to your inner attic, where your childhood dreams lie, going inside to the heart. Based on my over ten years research in the area of human development and leadership, here are ten easy steps you can take to awaken the Leader in you and rekindle your passion for greatness.

1. Humility. Leadership starts with humility. To be a highly successful leader, you must first humble yourself like a little child and be willing to serve others. Nobody wants to follow someone who is arrogant. Be humble as a child, always curious, always hungry and thirsty for knowledge. For what is excellence but knowledge plus knowledge plus knowledge - always wanting to better yourself, always improving, always growing. When you are humble, you become genuinely interested in people because you want to learn from them. And because you want to learn and grow, you will be a far more effective listener, which is the #1 leadership communication tool. When people sense you are genuinely interested in them, and listening to them, they will naturally be interested in you and listen to what you have to say.

2. SWOT Yourself. SWOT is an acronym for Strengths, Weaknesses, Opportunities, and Threats. Although it's a strategic management tool taught at Stanford and Harvard Business Schools and used by large multinationals, it can just as effectively be used in your own professional development as a leader. This is a useful key to gain access to self-knowledge, self-remembering, and self-honoring. Start by listing all your Strengths including your accomplishments. Then

write down all your Weaknesses and what needs to be improved. Make sure to include any doubts, anxieties, fears, and worries that you may have. These are the demons and dragons guarding the door to your inner attic. By bringing them to conscious awareness you can begin to slay them. Then proceed by listing all the Opportunities you see available to you for using your strengths. Finally, write down all the Threats or obstacles that are currently blocking you or that you think you will encounter along the way to achieving your dreams.

3. Follow Your Bliss. Regardless of how busy you are, always take time to do what you love doing. Being an alive and vital person vitalizes others. When you are pursuing your passions, people around you cannot help but feel impassioned by your presence. This will make you a charismatic leader. Whatever it is that you enjoy doing, be it writing, acting, painting, drawing, photography, sports, reading, dancing, networking, or working on entrepreneurial ventures, set aside time every week, ideally two or three hours a day, to pursue these activities. Believe me, you'll find the time. If you were to video tape yourself for a day, you would be shocked to see how much time goes to waste!

4. Dream Big. If you want to be larger than life, you need a dream that's larger than life. Small dreams won't serve you or anyone else. It takes the same amount of time to dream small than it does to dream big. So be Big and be Bold! Write down your One Biggest Dream. The one that excites you the most. Remember, don't be small and realistic; be bold and unrealistic! Go for the Gold, the Pulitzer, the Nobel, the Oscar, the highest you can possibly achieve in your field. After you ve written down your dream, list every single reason why you CAN achieve your dream instead of worrying about why you can't.

5. Vision. Without a vision, we perish. If you can't see yourself winning that award and feel the tears of triumph streaming down your face, it's unlikely you will be able to lead yourself or others to victory. Visualize what it would be like accomplishing your dream. See it, smell it, taste it, hear it, feel it in your gut.

6. Perseverance. Victory belongs to those who want it the most and stay in it the longest. Now that you have a dream, make sure you take consistent action every day. I recommend doing at least 5 things every day that will move you closer to your dream.

7. Honor Your Word. Every time you break your word, you lose power. Successful leaders keep their word and their promises. You can accumulate all the toys and riches in the world, but you only have one reputation in life. Your word is gold. Honor it.

8. Get a Mentor. Find yourself a mentor. Preferably someone who has already achieved a high degree of success in your field. Don't be afraid to ask. You've got nothing to lose. Mentors.ca is an excellent mentoring website and a great resource for finding local mentoring programs. They even have a free personal profile you can fill out in order to potentially find you a suitable mentor. In addition to mentors, take time to study autobiographies of great leaders that you admire. Learn everything you can from their lives and model some of their successful behaviors.

9. Be Yourself. Use your relationships with mentors and your research on great leaders as models or reference points to work from, but never copy or imitate them like a parrot. Everyone has vastly different leadership styles. History books are filled with leaders who are soft-spoken, introverted, and quiet, all the way to the other extreme of being out- spoken, extroverted, and loud, and everything in between. A quiet and simple

Gandhi or a soft-spoken peanut farmer named Jimmy Carter, who became president of the United States and won a Nobel Peace Prize, have been just as effective world leaders as a loud and flamboyant Churchill, or the tough leadership style employed by The Iron Lady, Margaret Thatcher. I admire Hemingway as a writer. But if I copy Hemingway, I'd be a second or third rate Hemingway, at best, instead of a first rate Sharif. Be yourself, your best self, always competing against yourself and bettering yourself, and you will become a first rate YOU instead of a second rate somebody else.

10. Give. Finally, be a giver. Leaders are givers. By giving, you activate a universal law as sound as gravity life gives to the giver, and takes from the taker. The more you give, the more you get. If you want more love, respect, support, and compassion, give love, give respect, give support, and give compassion. Be a mentor to others. Give back to your community. As a leader, the only way to get what you want, is by helping enough people get what they want first. As Sir Winston Churchill once said, "We make a living by what we get, we make a life by what we give."

Chapter 5

LIMITLESS MIND: UNCOVER YOUR FULL POTENTIAL

The Crucial Role of Your Thinking

What makes you different from everyone else? Is it your looks? Is it your interests or your hobbies?

Well, yes to an extent but more than anything else: it's your brain.

Your brain contains your memories, your goals, your desires, your beliefs and just about everything else that makes you 'who you are'. It's also what controls the way you think, the way you make plans and the way you react in any given situation.

It's the brain that makes the difference between your average Joe and Steve Jobs, Albert Einstein and Elon Musk. If you want to enjoy the kind of success, money and lifestyle of the world's most successful people then you need to think like them.

If you've been failing to get what you want out of life and if you've been feeling as though you're banging your head against the wall in your business, your relationships or your finances – then the problem almost certainly originates from your brain. The way you're thinking, your creativity, your intelligence... all of it comes from the physical make up of your brain and the way that you're approaching problems.

The best way to approach any problem is by approaching it at its root and at its most fundamental level. In almost every case the root is you: it starts and ends with you.

This book then is going to be the key to unlocking your full potential and to solving all your problems. It will help you achieve what you want and get what you want out of life by changing your thinking to be more in-line with the thinking of the world's most successful people.

This means two things:

- Looking at the thought processes of the world's most successful people – i.e. the way that they think that leads them to maximum success
- Looking at what you can do to change your brain, to break out of old habits and to

become more intelligent

In other words, you'll gain the tools and the ability to change the way you think, to change the way you approach problems and even to make yourself smarter. And once you can do that, then you can prime yourself to thrive in any given situation.

The Law of Attraction - What is it and Does it Work?

Let's start by looking at one fairly basic piece of advice when it comes to the way you think. This will serve as a nice opener that will show you just what a difference altering your thought patterns can make. We'll get onto the more advanced stuff further on, as well as how you can go about actually enforcing new thinking patters. For now though, let this be a nice little example.

What is the Law of Attraction?

The 'law of attraction' is a popular term that describes the process through which acting a certain way or holding certain beliefs can actually change your reality.

At its most basic level, the law of attraction states that 'as you think, so you become'. Likewise, as you become, so you become more.

But what on Earth does that mean?

Okay, let's take an example. If you wanted to become the youngest ever manager with the highest ever salary in the organization you work for, what would you do?

An excellent place to start would be to start believing you were already the top performing candidate in your organization and the most valuable member of your team. Believe it and live it and within a short amount of time it will happen.

Sounds too good to be true right? Well it actually makes a lot of sense once you get down to the mechanisms of how the process operates so read on and we'll get into the meat of it.

How the Law of Attraction Works

Have you ever noticed that money begets money? As in, the wealthier you are, the more easily you'll be able to accrue more wealth. Even if that just means investing your money, simply having cash means you have the means to have more cash.

The same thing goes for many aspects of life. For instance, if you have tons of nice stuff, you may well find that you acquire more nice stuff. Why? Because people will give you nicer things.

Again this doesn't seem to make sense until you break it down. Imagine you're giving a gift to someone super wealthy who has everything they could possibly want. What do you buy for the man or the woman who has everything? In order for your gift to be something they would want and something they would need, you'd have to get really creative and probably spend a ton of money meaning they'd get a really high quality gift.

This is why we give nicer and better things to people who already have tons of stuff. It's ironic really because it means that we buy nicer things for people who don't need them. The people who could do with a little extra nice stuff just get cheapo presents!

That is the law of attraction: like attracts like. If you want more of something, you need to get some of it – or you need to act as though you've already got it.

The Law of Attraction and Your Success

So how does this apply to career success?

Well, let's imagine you want to climb the ladder at your place of work and become the top performing member of staff on your team.

To do that, you would have to start believing you were already super successful and behaving that way as a result. This might mean getting a great haircut, dressing smarter, walking with your head held high, putting yourself forward for things and speaking with authority.

This is why people say things like 'dress for the job you want'. It makes a difference.

Can you see how that might help you to achieve more?

When you look confident and act like someone who is incredibly valuable, you will instantly inspire more faith in people. Your superiors will thus be more likely to put you up for important jobs, to consider you for career advancement and to give you praise and financial rewards. Likewise, the rest of your team would be more likely to defer to you and to come to you for advice (which your superiors would notice). You'd also take more risks owing to your inflated confidence and business is all about taking measured risks. You'd probably enjoy your job more too if you thought you were better at it, which would result in you being more productive, more engaged and more switched on.

Ever heard of a flow state? This is a neurochemical reaction that is characterized by the release of dopamine, norepinephrine, serotonin, anandamide and other neurotransmitters that help you feel focused, engaged and happy. When you believe in what you're doing, believe in yourself without doubts and are passionate about your job, you will get into this state much more often and more easily.

You'll even speak with more authority and present better.

By just believing you are the top dog in your organization you could transform yourself overnight from another employee into the hottest upcoming executive.

The Law of Attraction and Dating

This is even truer in the world of dating and it's something that pickup artists are highly aware of. If you want to thrive on the dating scene and really start playing above your league, then you need to make sure you believe you are an amazing catch. That alone will make you into the guy or girl who manages to attract anyone they want.

This is something we know intuitively. Studies show us that it's not looks that have the biggest impact on dating success but confidence.

That's because we all want to date someone who we think is a catch and who other people will think is a catch. We also want to date people who will protect our offspring and provide for our families in one way and another.

That means we need someone powerful. And people who act confident appear powerful.

One 'pickup artist' technique is something called 'peacocking'. Here you walk around with a funny hat on or a bright pink tie generally making an idiot of yourself. The reason this works is that it attracts attention but moreover it also makes you look confident. Why? Because someone with the guts to wear something so ridiculous must have reason to be confident and they must not be seeking approval from others. That means they must be 'top dog' and an alpha male or female.

Dating success is about looking the part and approaching people with an attractive confidence that sends the signal that 'yes, I am an amazing catch'.

The Problem With the Law of Attraction

That all sounds great doesn't it? Probably you're now thinking about ditching your old outfit, getting a haircut and practicing walking upright and speaking with authority. That way you can have a great career and a great love life and everything will fall into place.

That's great and all but it won't work. If it did, this would be a very short book...

Why? Because it needs to come from within. You need to actually believe the way you're acting and not just be acting.

This is the mistake that far too many people will make when they're trying to use the law of attraction to their advantage. People think that they can just start dressing smarter and making their voice sound deeper and louder and suddenly they'll get what they want. Too often than not, this results in nothing but embarrassment. Have you ever seen someone who is trying to be something they're not? Someone who wants so desperately to be 'slick' but who lacks the self-awareness to realize when that's not how they're coming across?

We've all seen people who brag about how much they drink, who try to act cocky around us and who flash their cash around... but who everyone else just feels kind of embarrassed for. It isn't pretty and it's also a pretty good way to get your front teeth knocked out.

That's the thing. People can really tell the difference between someone who is genuinely confident, powerful and full of self-belief versus someone who is play acting. In order to truly succeed you need to actually believe – not just act like you do.

That will come later on though, don't worry!

Positivity, Making Your Own Luck and Taking MASSIVE Action

First though, let's take another look at an example of how the right mindset can make you super successful. This time we're going to talk about something that Tony Robbins talks about all the time: taking MASSIVE action. We'll also look at how you 'make your own luck' and why you really can't fail.

By the end of this chapter you'll start to see the steps you need to take to succeed but you'll also see why you're the only person who is holding yourself back.

Why You Can't Fail

If you want something badly enough, you really can't fail. All you need to do is to believe in yourself, play the odds and take massive action.

Oh... okay then... thanks... What does any of that mean?

Well, one interpretation of 'massive action' is just 'doing something to a huge extent'. As in, giving it 100%, putting your all into it and doing everything you can to make it happen. It means being completely unreserved and creating a huge quantity of work, effort or whatever else it is.

Do you think that right now, you could become a hugely successful Kindle author? And make a living from writing eBooks?

Nah, that's impossible right? Only a very few people can achieve that kind of success from Amazon.

Okay then, well try this:

Learn how to write fast. As in, learn how to churn out 5-10,000 words a day. That's very do-able and I know that because I do it all the time. In fact I will often write 20-30,000 words a day. Granted I couldn't do it when I first started, I had to build up to it. But in time,

I learned how to get to those 20- 30,000 daily.

Now you can do that, you can write on average one Kindle book a day. Kindle books do tend to be about 10,000 words.

So now you're publishing a Kindle book daily and you're selling each one for maybe $5. That's really reasonable, so it's the kind of price that people could make an impulse purchase on.

In 365 days, you'll have 365 Kindle books on the store. Within three years you could have about a thousand books on the Kindle Store.

Woah.

And seeing as the books will likely rank higher over time, this will mean that you'll start earning more money the longer you keep them there. Especially if they're good and they got good reviews. And if you chose smart niches (topics) with compelling titles this will help too.

Now imagine that you're selling 10% of those titles, one a day. After three years you'll be making about $100-300 a day. Woah.

And chances are, with that many books out, one or two of them will gain momentum and become runaway hits. It's not impossible to think that you could easily be earning $500 or more daily. And at this point you would have to do no work at all.

In six years you could have 2,000 books on the Kindle store and you'd be almost unable to fail. You could also start pumping some of your profits back into marketing and you could sell those eBooks in other ways too – on ClickBank, through a landing page, through eBay, via LuLu (a self- publishing platform), on iTunes... the possibilities are endless. And once that many books were written, you wouldn't have to put in any more work – the money would just come in all on its own.

So that's it: a completely foolproof plan to becoming a millionaire through Kindle books. Sure, there's a chance it wouldn't work... but you have to admit it's small.

And there are similar approaches you could take in almost every area of your life. Imagine if you put that kind of effort into your current career, into a website, into a mobile app, or into your relationships. When you take massive action you really can't fail.

But you won't. Why? Because it's too risky.

Honestly, who's going to give up their job for three years on a whim? Who's going to take out a loan from the bank or from Mum and Dad to lock themselves away and write 3,000 eBooks? You could do it in 8 hours a day and hold a part-time job... there are workarounds... but the commitment and the risk is huge.

And that means that you have to 100%, without a doubt, believe in what it is that you're doing in order to start making money. This is where most people fall down.

It's the same problem with working out. If I told you that you could have an amazing ripped six pack, huge biceps and incredible physical prowess and all you had to do was follow a set training regime what would happen? It might sound appealing but chances are that you would give up after the first week.

And why?

Because after the first week you might find that you didn't yet have the incredible physique you hoped to have. And so you would give up on it, thinking 'it didn't work'. It's a lot of evenings to give up and a lot of time to sacrifice if you don't think it's going to work.

If you genuinely believed though that you would get the outcome you wanted, you would probably do anything to make it happen. So to change your strategy and your outcome, you need to change your belief first.

We Make Our Own Luck

This is an example of how we make our own luck. When you take massive action you skew the odds heavily in your favor and luck becomes very much on your side.

But you don't have to go that far to start making your own luck. In fact, all you have to do is to just believe in what you're doing a little more and just take a few more chances.

I knew someone who was a successful mobile app developer. They created a mobile app that made them in excess of $30,000 in one year and it's gone on to make the same every year since – on top of their existing salary.

Nice.

Everyone then went ahead and told that person: 'man,

you're really talented!' and generally to shower them with praise. They never saw it though: they said their secret was just to keep trying. They had released 20 apps prior to that, none of which made more than a few sales but the success of that last one was the result simply of getting a good review on a big website that drove tons of downloads their way.

They took a 'fail fast' approach, meaning that they created MVPs (Minimally Viable Products) and released them quickly to see if there was a market out there for those apps. When something didn't work, they just moved on.

Again, by taking lots of chances, they made their own luck. Luck is probability and the more you try, the better your chances of success will be.

Of course to take lots of chances though you again need to believe they will pay off. You need to be positive and optimistic enough to take the risk. And you need to have the thick skin necessary to be able to face defeat, pick yourself up and try again.

Changing Your Focus

Another way you can make your own luck is simply to change your focus. What does this mean? Well, it means that you are focusing on different things.

Positive people have been shown in studies to be 'luckier' than negative people and there are a ton of reasons for that.

Here's a fun little experiment that lots of self-help gurus use to demonstrate the power of focus.

What you're going to do is to look around the room and to try and see everything that you can that's green. Keep looking around and make note of plants, people's coats – anything that is green in color. Do that for a minute then return to reading this... Okay, you back? Good. Now tell me everything you saw that was red.

Ha, got you! But it's not just a cruel trick, it's actually an example of how you only see what you're looking for. If you look again you'll probably find there's tons of stuff that's red in the room and you probably missed about 90% of it in your quest for finding green things.

Some people will even find things that 'aren't there' when they're looking hard enough – did you count something burgundy as red?

You see, you find whatever it is you're looking for. And that's one way in which you make your own luck.

If you are someone who is positive and optimistic then you will be more likely to be looking out for opportunities and that quite simply means you'll be more likely to find them.

What's Holding You Back?

A lack of positivity isn't the only thing that can hold you back though. Rather you'll find that it likely comes down to some pretty deep psychology and even neuroses.

For most people, the idea of taking massive action, of putting it all on the line and of committing to a goal or idea is something that makes them want to curl up and put their head in the sand.

The problem is that giving anything 100% means exposing yourself and that means making yourself vulnerable. And too many of us are just too afraid to do that. This is why people will create a website that they hope will be their big money maker that lets them live their dreams...

And then they'll go ahead and promptly not tell anyone about it because they're embarrassed. Your personal network on Facebook provides you with an excellent place to start marketing – your friends want you to succeed and will probably spread it to their contacts if you ask them to. But you don't because you're embarrassed. And the result is that you miss out on that huge marketing opportunity.

If you're too shy to announce your plans to your own friends what chance do you have?

It's also why people will create a blog and then post to it every week or every other week. You really think you can make a blog your primary source of income by posting every other week? If you want your blog to become your full time career then you should be treating it like it already is your full time career. Remember that law of attraction? And that means that you should be posting their ten times daily with new, lengthy, well- researched posts and then spending ages promoting every single one of those posts everywhere you can. Do that and once again you can't help but succeed. You could at least do it at the weekends!

And this is DEFINITELY why people:

- Don't go to gyms
- Don't join classes
- Don't put themselves forward and network
- Don't communicate properly with their partners

- Don't sign up to dating sites

- Don't approach people in bars

- Don't ask for promotions...

Honestly, how can you expect to succeed when you're too afraid to try?

How many people do you know who tell you over and over again that they have this amazing business idea but they spend so long perfecting it that they never actually take it live? These people are not only scared of failure but they're scared of what failure will do to them emotionally. They'd rather not release their dream project at all (and know it won't be successful) than release it and risk getting a negative reaction. 99% of people are quite frankly deluded when it comes to this kind of thing.

And some of us simply don't get round to things because we're just too tired and exhausted and drained. Sure, you could pick up that phone and offer your services to someone in your neighborhood... but it should does sound like a lot of effort doesn't it? You could go and hit the gym, but it would be easier to just lie here a little longer first.

Yep, good luck making your mark on the world with an attitude like that!

As you can see, all that stuff that these productivity gurus talk about really is true. There's actually nothing stopping you from achieving what you want and if you know how to write a good plan then you really can't fail. The problem is that we get in our own way, we talk ourselves out of things and we remain in our little bubble of routine. Oh dear.

You are different though. There's one thing that sets you apart from everyone else. And you know what that is? You are taking the time to read this book!

How to Write and Stick to Goals - Creating a Plan of Action

By now you've hopefully come to the conclusion that you need to start doing things difficulty. If you've been shying away from risk and wallowing in self-pity/low energy, it's time for a change. If you've been putting off going after the things that you really want and instead just going 'with the flow' because it's easier... then again you need to change.

One of the best ways to do that is to begin with a plan. You need to know what it is you want and you need to know how it is you're going to achieve it.

Thinking Outside the Box

Once again, let's start by reiterating that you really don't need to shy away from the big stuff. You can make pretty much anything happen if you put your mind to it simply by taking that massive action and having the right strategy.

Sometimes that strategy though involves taking a slightly different approach from usual. For instance, you might not have thought about releasing a thousand Kindle books as a good way to make money online. But by coming at your objective from the easiest angle with the least resistance you can overcome the odds and succeed where others might have failed.

A great example of someone else doing this is Sylvester Stallone, the actor, bodybuilder, painter, entrepreneur and all-round polymath.

Don't let Sly's muscles and drawl fool you, he is actually an incredibly smart, driven and inspirational guy. When he decided he wanted to be a famous actor you see, he took a completely different route than most people by leveraging one of his biggest skills: writing.

Sly had been acting in bit parts and even soft porn for years and made no headway in the industry. At the time in fact he was close to living on the streets and even had to sell his dog.

That's when he wrote the script for Rocky and started showing it to directors and producers. As the legend goes, one company liked the script so much that they were willing to pay him a huge amount of money for it – which would end all of his financial troubles.

But Stallone stayed steadfast and instead said that he just wanted to star in the movie. He refused all kinds of offers and remained completely rigid on the deal that if Hollywood executives wanted his script, they'd have to cast him in the movie.

Of course they eventually agreed, he bought back his dog and the rest is history.

The point is that Sly overcame tremendous odds by making a plan and taking a different route into the industry.

Today there's more ways than ever for you to do this. Say you want to become a Hollywood star... what could you do to make that happen? Of course you could move to LA, hire an agent and go to auditions like everyone else. Or you could try going Stallone's route by writing your own vehicle and offering to star in it.

Or you could do something completely different. For instance, you could create your own YouTube channel making amateur movies every week (teaming up with hobbyist film makers) and eventually you would probably generate a fan base and a following and Hollywood would come-a- knocking.

Or you could take to Kickstarter and get a film made that way. Or you could become a day trader, get super rich and then buy your own production company.

Here's a question: how do you go about launching your own space project and walking on the moon? That's a goal that sounds impossible right? Well, it's also something that one entrepreneur – Peter Diamandis – has taken great strides towards. How did he do that? By taking the 'line of super credibility'.

Basically, Peter launched the 'X-Prize Foundation' which awarded a huge cash prize to any company that could build a commercial craft capable of space travel. He didn't have the skills himself but by using this strategy, he motivated those that did have the resources to move towards the goal he set for them.

There was another problem though: he also didn't have the money. How does a guy with no money, no authority and no business in space travel motivate big businesses to invest time and effort into such an unbelievable task?

Simple: he took the line of 'super credibility'. What that meant was that when he announced his prize – before he even had the money to put behind him – he did so by going on stage with a bunch of former astronauts and leaders in the industry. Because those people were there that meant that everyone believed in what he had to say. Those people provided the 'super credibility' and they changed him from being 'some dreamer' to someone who appeared to have the means. The cash money then came from various backers following that announcement. But the point is that this was one guy with a dream who used a smart strategy to help push forwards the pursuit of commercial space travel. That's an incredible story of success and it really should tell you that you can accomplish anything.

If you're smart about it.

The trick then is to make a plan that you completely believe in – which means assessing what your skills are, what your resources are, who your contacts are and what's achievable in the shortest amount of time.

Later in this book we will be talking about something called 'functional fixedness' in regards to creative thinking. You might want to refer to that when coming up with your plan.

Minimizing Risk

What's also important when creating a plan of action is to minimize your risk.

We've talked already about how people tend to talk themselves out of taking action for fear of putting themselves on the line and due to the risk aversion that we all experience.

Throughout this book we'll be largely focusing on how you can change your thinking with regards to risk aversion, so that you can overcome it and make it a thing of the past. In the meantime though, we'll also be approaching this from another angle: by removing the risk in the first place.

To create a plan that you're actually likely to stick to, you need to find ways that you can remove the elements of risk that are currently putting you off.

Because if you're smart you see, there needn't be any risk with a lot of different projects.

For instance, many people will put off changing jobs even when they're very unhappy with the place they work. Their boss might be breathing down their neck, they might feel that the work they do isn't rewarding and they might feel that they aren't listened to or respected in the workplace. Bearing in mind what a huge proportion of our lives we spend at work, this is enough to make pretty much anyone completely miserable and it's something you should certainly seek to change.

The problem is that when someone suggests that these people change their jobs, they will freeze up. They can't leave their job! What if they don't find another one? What if they then end up with no money? Who is going to pay the rent? Where will their children sleep?

But no one said they had to quit their job. You don't have to leave a job in order to start looking for other jobs, you just need to start applying for other jobs in the evenings. You don't leave your current place of work until you've got something else lined up. That way there is zero risk.

The same goes for starting your own business. Say you want to start selling computer equipment instead of working your current job but you're too afraid to leave your work. What do you do?

Simple: you buy some wholesale items at a low price, then you start trying to sell them on eBay or through your own website. Once you manage that, you invest some of that profit into more stock. You send out the deliveries in the evening and you keep your inventory in your basement. Over time your turnover will increase and so will your profits and it's only once you have a stable income that you need to leave your job.

And it doesn't just apply to business. How do you minimize risk when it comes to meeting members of the opposite sex? The risk here is that you get laughed at, turned away or generally have your feelings trampled on. It doesn't sound like a big deal but it's more than enough to prevent a lot of people from going ahead and introducing themselves to that hottie over at the bar.

So to minimize risk, try not going over. Instead, find a spot where you're comfortable and relax with a drink in your hand. Now look round the bar for people you like. When you find someone who looks attractive and pleasant, just try smiling at them or even winking at them.

If they're at all interested, they will smile or wink back and that will give you the permission you need to go over. They may even come over to you! But if they don't, then what you need to do instead is to just move on and find someone else. This way there's no risk – you haven't even gone over there so they can't 'turn you down'. The worst outcome is that nothing happens. Zero risk. And what's better, is that this strategy also allows you to play the numbers game. You can wink at a thousand girls or guys in one night, starting from the ones you're most interested in and moving your way down. Eventually one of them is bound to be receptive and that way you can quickly and efficiently find where to spend most of your time.

Online dating is also great because it's so risk free – the only worry is that you might end up wasting time sifting through people who don't respond to your attempts at contact. Here's a quick solution to that: try outsourcing it to your friends and family. They're always poking their nose into your love life anyway, so why not use that to your advantage?

Identifying Your Goals

Hopefully as you read this, you're starting to get ideas for ways to approach your own goals – ways that will be more efficient and more risk free and that will make the unachievable seem... achievable.

There's just one problem though: which might be the fact that you don't know what it is you want to achieve. Don't worry if this is the way you feel, it's the case for countless people and it's actually quite normal.

Some of us are fortunate enough to know exactly what it is we want to be from the day we turn 10 and can then work on perfectly executing that plan at every step of the way.

But what about the rest of us who want abstract things and can't quite put our goals and ambitions into words?

A few things can help you to try and define what it is you want from life:

- Look at your role models – Look at the people you admire most and think about what it is that they all have in common

- Think about the things you would change in your life right now – Instead of starting from scratch and coming up with a 'vision' instead try looking at specific things about your life that you would change right now

- Imagine your happy place – Imagine your happy place and what your vision of success is. Where are you? What are you doing? It might be that you're on a sunny beach somewhere in a mansion – in which case it would seem you need money.

- Think about the essence of your goals – In some rare cases you might have multiple goals or you might have goals that are genuinely unattainable. If you want to be a T-Rex for instance, then you're in trouble (for Will Ferrell fans, that was indeed a *Step Brothers* reference). In these cases though, think instead about what the 'essence' of that ambition is. Do you want to be a T-Rex or do you want to be powerful? Do you want to own your own business, or do you want respect? Do you want to be an astronaut or do you want adventure?

- Think about what it is that you wanted to do as a child, often that's still what you want you've just been taught to deny yourself those more childish sounding objectives.

- Imagine your own eulogy and what you would want people to say about you. How do you want to be remembered when you're gone?
- Imagine what advice you would give to someone who was in exactly your position. What would you tell them to focus on or to fix?
- Think about when you were last happiest – What was it that made you so happy and how can you recreate that?

The most important thing during this process is to be completely honest with yourself. Don't leave out the things you think are unrealistic or you'll just be lying to yourself. You want to be a superhero? Great: that's what you're going to work with.

At the same time, don't worry if your goals don't fall neatly into a box or if you can't easily outline them on paper. You might find that you have 20 goals, or that your goal isn't very exciting. Maybe your goal is to have a really big garden. Great. That's a great goal – go with it. Don't try and change your goals to fit other people's expectations. Go with what you know will make you happiest. Your goal might be completely and utterly weird – maybe you want to recreate a level from Sonic the Hedgehog in your back garden. Go for it! No one knows what the meaning of life is and as such there is no right or wrong answer regarding the way you choose to live yours. Be free to go after whatever it is that you want.

Likewise, don't worry if your goal isn't anything to do with your career. That's actually a good thing – you don't have to define yourself by your job.

And stop worrying about 'being too old' (the cause of so many mid-life crises). As the old saying goes, 'it's never too late to be what you've always wanted to be'. In fact, often being older can be an advantage. Want to be an actor? Great! There are tons of bit parts for older actors and you'll have the spare time to go to lots of auditions. Want to live somewhere sunny?

Being retired means you should have the funds and the lack of ties to make this possible. Want to be a rock star? Take that YouTube route – it's pretty easy to imagine a geriatric electric guitarist going viral.

Don't overcomplicate matters either, or take unnecessarily difficult routes to get to where you want to be. If every time you close your eyes you imagine yourself on a yacht somewhere sunny then you need to be a millionaire right? Wrong: all you need is to move to a sunny country and then invest all your disposable income into a yacht. Sound reckless? Not if it is genuinely what will make you happy.

Of course you do need to think about the mitigating factors like your family. Perhaps your partner doesn't want to move country. This does complicate matters and it's fine to feel tugged in multiple directions – you just need to slightly alter your plan.

Your plan doesn't even have to be a static thing. People change with time and so do our objectives. If you find that you don't have a concrete 'dream' right now then use the advice in this book to focus on just changing small things that will make you happier. You can add more to that plan as you go.

Having the Plan is All That Matters

What's really important though, is recognizing the importance of simply having a plan and having a goal. It actually doesn't matter all that much whether your goal works or not. What's important is simply that you go ahead and try.

That might sound like the moral that belongs at the end of a Disney movie but it's actually true.

You can be anything you want to be. It's only being successful that's hard.

Want to be a writer? Then start writing – congratulations, you are now a writer!

Want to be a rock musician? Then start playing music on YouTube – congratulations, you are now a rock musician!

Sure, you might not be professional and you might not be making a living but you're still doing what you love and you can still get a lot of meaning and happiness from that. Having a goal gives life meaning, direction and purpose and it means that you will no longer be defining yourself by your 9- 5.

When someone at a party asks you about yourself, do you tell them your job as the main point? Is that 'what you do'? Is it 'who you are'? Instead, tell them about your side project. That's what should really get you going and that should tell them a lot more about who you are and where your passions lie.

If you take nothing else from this book, then just focus on this one message: start trying.

How to Think Like a Successful Person

Now you've gotten all that through your head, you'll hopefully have started coming up with your plan of action. This is what will make the path to your success (as in the way that you define success) easiest. By following that plan you should minimize the time and effort you invest, the amount of risk involved and your chances of failure.

You also know at this point that you now need to believe in that plan and yourself and make your own luck if you're going to succeed. This is what makes the difference between those entrepreneurial types and those 'over achievers' versus everyone else.

Cognitive Behavioral Therapy to Change Your Thought Patterns

That's the second piece of the puzzle but it might also be the stumbling block for many people. How do you go about breaking out of your current thought patterns and adopting the thinking of those people who are highly successful?

Unfortunately if you're just as pessimistic as everyone else and if your ambitions have typically been modest and 'realistic' (what a despicable word) then you will have been 'practicing' and thus reinforcing negative thought patterns your whole life. It's thus going to take some real effort to break out of those and to start thinking in a more positive and success- oriented manner.

This is where CBT comes in.

What is CBT?

CBT stands for 'Cognitive Behavioral Therapy'. This is a psychotherapeutic technique used by therapists and psychologists to treat all kinds of mental health problems – and phobias, anxieties and stress in particular.

What's interesting about CBT is that it's also a technique you can use on your own. One of the reasons it has become so popular with the NHS in the UK, is that it doesn't require anyone to be physically present. Other forms of therapy like psychotherapy require lengthy sessions lasting hours multiple times a week. CBT on the other hand can be conducted via e-mail and actually has much more evidence in support of its effectiveness as well.

The general idea behind CBT then is to give patients the tools they need to reprogram their thoughts and to change the way they think. Therapists use this to teach people how to get rid of phobias or OCD – but we can use it as well to try and model our brains after those of the most successful people. And also just to make sure that we are sticking to our goals and objectives.

How it Works

To do CBT you first have to identify the contents of your thoughts. From there, you then have to assess them as being constructive or maladaptive and then replace them/eliminate them where necessary. You can then also use various different exercises and strategies in order to cement these positive effects.

Two important stages in this process are mindfulness and cognitive restructuring.

Mindfulness

In mindfulness, you will essentially be listening to your own thoughts and assessing them. This is a form of meditation but unlike transcendental meditation where you are trying to quieten your thoughts and block them out, here you are simply becoming an observer of your own brain and identifying the thoughts you have as they pass by.

Mindfulness can be practiced as an intentional form of meditation where you are actively listening to your thoughts. At the same time though, it can also be used in a more casual manner or a more passive manner. For instance, it might mean simply thinking back to the last time you were in a certain position and asking yourself now what was on your mind at that time. Likewise, it might mean simply being partly aware of your own thoughts in any given situation. Just make sure that you are monitoring your thoughts one way or another.

If you had a phobia of heights, you would then use mindfulness in order to identify the thoughts that caused this fear which might include things like 'I'm going to fall' or 'I want to jump'. These of course only cause you to get worse when really you should be thinking positive affirmations like 'I'm in complete control' or 'the railings will stop me from falling'. In the case of fulfilling your goals and thinking like a more successful person, you'll need to identify the negative self-talk and replace that with statements about why you can't fail.

Cognitive Restructuring

Cognitive restructuring is the term used for the second part of the process whereby you change the thoughts you've identified as problematic. There are furthermore two ways you might go about this called thought challenging and hypothesis testing.

Thought Challenging:

Thought challenging essentially means that you are asking yourself just how realistic your current concerns are. So for instance, if you find yourself thinking 'I'm going to end up on the streets' you might challenge that thought simply by assessing how realistic it really is.

Are you really likely to end up on the street? Or is it the case that you would probably be offered support by your partner, your Mum or your sister? How long would it realistically take you to completely run out of funds? In that time, wouldn't you be able to get another job – possibly better than the one you had before? At the very least, wouldn't you be able to get a part time job in a supermarket? Move somewhere cheaper to live?

Rent a room in a shared house?

9/10 of our fears really aren't that realistic and aren't founded on much. Challenge their logic and you might find that you have nothing to worry about.

Hypothesis Testing

Hypothesis testing is the process of actually testing those illogical thoughts. So say you're afraid of approaching women or men in bars, you might use thought challenging and tell yourself that it's actually very rare that anyone should make a scene and even if they did it probably wouldn't be the end of the world – does it matter what strangers in a bar think?

Problem is though, you're probably not going to really believe that until you actually test it yourself. That means you need to try approaching people to test your fear that you're going to get shot down. What you'll find is that it doesn't happen, that you're fine and that you learn over time that there's nothing to be afraid of.

Hypothesis testing is absolutely great for anyone who has any kind of social anxiety – especially because it also serves as a form of 'training' for overcoming nerves. All you have to do is to pick the situation where failure really doesn't matter. Try going into a shop where you don't know anyone and where you never shop. Now, when you buy something, try putting on a stupid accent, stuttering and being generally weird and awkward. You'll find that before you approach the shop, your heart starts racing and that you feel completely pumped and anxious. This is normal.

But when you do it, you'll find the shop owner probably doesn't even comment on your odd behavior. They assume you have mental health problems, serve you and then let you go about your business.

What you learn in this process is that you can get away with a lot more weirdness and awkwardness than you realize and that people are actually just really polite. That then gives you free reign to be bold, to be daring, to be out there and to network. And as you practice you will get your fight or flight response under control such that it's not a problem anymore. If this seems a little scary at first, then try finding a buddy to do it with.

Fear Setting

'Fear setting' is a technique suggested by the one and only Tim Ferris in his book The Four Hour Workweek. Here he outlines a process that is essentially a form of

CBT as applied to entrepreneurialism, business and self-development.

The idea is simply to clearly define your fears and to write them down on paper. Write down every single reason you have for talking yourself into not doing X and not doing Y. Now go through all those things and break each one down. Analyze how likely each of those things is to actually happen and then write down a contingency plan that outlines how you would deal with the problem if it were to occur. The objective here is to remove the 'power' from each of your fears so that you feel ready to completely execute your plan.

Some More Strategies

Some other good strategies you can use include those that revolve around priming yourself and removing bad habits that cause negative thoughts.

Priming by the way simply means putting yourself into a state of mind where you can win. Here are a few CBT-esque techniques you could consider adopting:

Positive Affirmations

Positive affirmations are positive statements you repeat to encourage yourself. The idea here is simply to make your positive thoughts become the 'habit' instead of your negative ones. To help yourself remember these, try using post-it notes and putting them up around your house.

Power Positions

Simply standing in a victory stance (arms over your head) puts you in a state of 'win' and producing hormones associated with drive and success. Try it in the bathroom next time you're going to an interview.

Body language

Moreover, make sure you have your body language straight. This might mean just pointing your chest up at the ceiling and imagine a beam of light coming out of it and getting in the habit of doing this every time you step through a door. It completely changes the way you feel and makes a much better first impression.

Priming

You can also prime yourself directly by listening to motivating music or watching motivating films. Better yet, remind yourself every day of all the things you've done that you're proud of and all the times you've succeeded. This way you can set yourself into a state where you're feeling successful, proud and on top of the world and as we've discussed this will ensure that people automatically view you as being all those things to a greater extent.

How Does Counseling Differ From Cognitive Therapies Such As NLP Or CBT?

Counseling involves meeting with a counselor and having the opportunity to explore via talking, difficulties you may be having or distress you may be experiencing. The counselors role is to listen attentively to what you are telling them in order to begin to form an understanding of your perspective of the difficulties you may be experiencing. Counseling does not involve giving advice or guiding a client to take a particular course of action. Through the process of being listened to by a counselor, who is trained to reflect and help you to clarify your problem, counseling can be a way of enabling change, more choices or of helping you release strong emotion and feeling, which you have kept bottled up or have felt unable to share with family or friends.

During counseling you are able to explore and talk freely about any aspect of your life, be it past, present or in the future, in a setting which is confidential.

Counselors accept and respect their clients and provide a safe environment for the client to explore their life, relationships and themselves. Counseling can be very useful for helping people to deal with distressing emotions associated with bereavement and loss. Counseling can be very useful for you if you feel you would benefit from being listened to or feel burdened by troubles.

Cognitive approaches such as CBT and NLP are both approaches used to promote positive change in individuals. Like counseling, the therapist will treat you with respect and provide a confidential environment for you to work through your problems. Cognitive approaches are effective at alleviating emotional distress and behavioural problems. Unlike counseling, cognitive techniques can be practised by the individual and are based on the philosophy that the content of our thoughts have a major influence on our emotions and behaviour. Through cognitive therapy, it is possible to learn ways to eradicate or manage the types of thoughts you have, which means that the state of mind they sustain, such as anxiety, can be resolved. CBT and NLP are solution-focused techniques that focus on the 'here and now'. Unlike other talking treatments, such as counseling, the focus is not on trying to find the cause of your distress (the therapist will take a full history and discuss your past but practical strategies to promote well-being in the present is the main focus) rather you will learn to improve your state of mind right now. This involves learning which factors maintain your distress or problem and learning strategies to overcome your problem which you will practice in your own time.

NLP is an intimidating name for what is a common sense, practical and effective therapy. 'Neuro' means brain, 'linguistic' relates to how we use language both to communicate with others, and within our own brain and 'programming' relates to how we create and use patterns of behaviour in everyday life in order to get results. We know that we experience the world through our senses and that this information is translated into thoughts. How you use this internal language in your own brain directly affects your physiology, emotions and behaviour. People tend to develop habits and patterns of using internal language that have positive or negative effects on their emotions and behaviour. NLP therapy, Hert encourages new perspectives and options in thinking, giving you more choices about your behavior and emotions, enhancing your communication and relationships and generating lasting life skills.

Cognitive Behavioural Therapy focuses on how you think about a problem (cognitive) and what you do about it (behaviour). CBT can teach you how to recognise and change faulty thinking patterns. This doesn't mean that you will always think positive thoughts. It is a way to gain control over racing repetitive thoughts, which feed anxiety and depression. CBT can help you make sense of overwhelming problems by breaking them down into achievable parts.

Both these therapy approaches are practical and focused on problem solving in order to meet your therapy goals. This means that unlike counseling, sessions are more structured and less free flowing as you move towards change with the support of your therapist. Often people will seek cognitive therapy such as CBT, Herts or NLP, Herts, when they want solutions to their problem or to move on from limiting thinking, feelings or behaviour.

The Neuroscience of Intelligence and How to Hack Your Brain

Using these techniques, you'll have made yourself far more likely to succeed by changing the way you approach problems, the way you view yourself and more.

But how about becoming smarter? Can you hack your way to actually being more intelligent? Because that really does play a role too...

This is a huge topic and not something we can completely cover here but this little primer should give you a bit of an idea of how your brain works and whether or not it can be changed.

You Are Your Connectome

Your connectome is the huge web of neurons (brain cells) that make up your brain. You have billions of these neurons and they essentially would look like the most complicated mind map in the world were you to try and draw it all out.

This connectome is what contains your ideas, your memories, your beliefs and just about everything else and it grows and changes all the time.

Whenever you see something, remember something or experience something, a neuron fires and sends a message to the neurons around it across a 'synapse' (gap). When two neurons fire at the same time, they gradually form a connection and the more often this association is reinforced the more the two will be connected. This is why you can train a dog to salivate when you ring a bell – because 'neurons that fire together, wire together'. This process is called 'brain plasticity'.

Another thing also affects how effectively different neurons wire together though too. Specifically that's your neurotransmitters. Neurotransmitters are chemicals in the brain of which there are over 100 and which aid the synaptic transmissions (action potentials). The main ones are dopamine, serotonin, norepinephrine and acetylcholine. These neurotransmitters regulate our memory and attention among other things – dopamine makes things seem important for instance, as does norepinephrine, which is why increasing these chemicals via caffeine makes us more focused and improves our memory.

What is Intelligence?

Defining intelligence is somewhat problematic. There is a difference between fluid intelligence (which is your ability to process information) versus crystalized information (which is your knowledge). Meanwhile some people will be excellent at math, while other people will be more creative and others will be better at debating – but the skills do not necessarily correlate.

Ultimately though, a lot of our skill is the result of our brain's ability to adapt to the demands we place on it. This is often referred to as 'SAID' – Specific Adaptation to Imposed Demands. Intelligence and skill is simply the result of practice + adaptability along with the right chemicals to enhance focus and speed.

Creativity meanwhile seems to be our brain's ability to make connections between seemingly unrelated ideas in order to find new combinations of ideas.

Can You Improve Intelligence?

So with all that in mind, how do you improve creativity and intelligence?

One strategy would be to increase your brain's adaptability and then to practice using it. To increase adaptability, you need to increase those neurotransmitters associated with attention and awareness. The best way to do this is by getting plenty of amino acids in your diet. Why? Because amino acids are the natural precursors to neurotransmitters – the place that our brain gets the raw building blocks. Amino acids come from proteins, so these are especially important for boosting brain power. Likewise, you should consume lots of omega 3 fatty acid from fish and nuts because it encourages cell membrane permeability meaning that your brain cells can communicate more easily. Vitamins and minerals are also crucial for maintaining your neurochemical cocktail – zinc, magnesium, B vitamins and C vitamins in particular. Ultimately the goal should be to eat nutrient dense foods.

On top of this, you also need to make sure you get plenty of exercise which will encourage neurogenesis (the creation of new brain cells) as well as helping oxygen get to the brain providing it with more energy. Sleep is also very important for forming new neural connections as it's when our brain cements much of what we learned during the day. Many people in a quest to boost their brain function will take all kinds of crazy supplements but not focus on the basics – like going to bed an hour earlier which is a thousand times more effective.

Can you become more intelligent? That's up for debate. But eating a nutrient rich diet high in protein, exercising, sleeping and using your brain are all things you can do to have a big impact.

20 Common Traits and Behaviors of Highly Successful People

To end with, let's take a look at 20 of the most common traits and behaviors shared by the world's most successful people. You can then try to emulate these to try and encourage that correlation to work for you...

1. Optimism: We've already discussed why this is important and it's very self-evident when you speak to any of the world's biggest achievers. They all have a sense of optimism and happiness.

2. Risk Taking: Likewise, successful people appear to be risk taking. Higher risks have higher rewards and if you don't try, you don't know. There is a bell curve here though: if you're too risk taking then it can go the other way. And extreme risk taking is actually associate with psychopathy... Take risks but pick and choose your risks carefully.

3. Hardiness: Hardiness is the ability to take hits and bounce back. It's what gets you to keep trying even when things look bad and when people are telling you to give up. If you don't give up, then you haven't failed.

4. Creativity: Creativity is a crucial skill for coming up with new ideas and solutions to problems. Creativity tends to be highest when you're most relaxed, so make sure you are regularly taking time out to chill and you should increase your creative juices.

5. Resourcefulness: High achievers are resourceful meaning that they can make the most of the things they have available to them – like Tony Stark who builds the Iron Man suit while in a cave. The trick to resourcefulness is to overcome 'functional fixedness'. Stop thinking of things as tools and think of them as materials. You don't just have a hammer: you have a hammer, you have metal and you have wood. Those are a lot more resources.

6. Networking: Very few people genuinely succeed to a huge extent completely on their own. You need to be willing to put yourself out there and to form a team with people who can help you make your ambitions a reality.

7. Passion: Passion is crucial for success. If you want to be highly successful then you need to

pick something you love doing so that you feel as though you're never really working – you're just doing what you were born to do. This will come across in everything you do. It will even make you gesticulate more which is the secret to appearing charismatic.

8. Gratitude: If you were really successful already… how would you know it? Gratitude means being thankful for what you have already and many successful people count their blessing each morning as a matter of habit to encourage this trait.

9. Exercise: Exercise boosts intelligence and it teaches you to stick at goals.

10. Meditation: Tim Ferris interviews some of the most successful people in the world on his podcast and something they almost all have in common is that they meditate.

11. Questioning: Steve Jobs said that the secret to success is to just keep asking 'why doesn't it work?'

12. Positive Affirmations: Positive affirmations are a tool you can use to bolster success. Like meditation this is a technique that many successful people say they use.

13. Sleep: Successful people recognize the importance of sleep. Don't ignore this at any cost.

14. Curiosity: That constant questioning comes from curiosity and likewise being curious is what will drive you to learn, to experiment and test. And that's how you make breakthroughs.

15. Drive: Successful people are driven and they are self-starters. That means their drive comes from inside and is not reliant on the approval of others. You won't succeed until you're willing to put in the hours, get up at the crack of dawn and weather the storm.

16. Integrity: Passion and integrity go hand in hand and if you want to be successful then you can't cut corners or deliver a shoddy product. People who cheat almost always get their comeuppance and if you're tempted to try and swindle people, it means you're not in the right line of work. You need integrity and you need professional pride to succeed.

17. Patience: Success doesn't come overnight and it's all too easy to get bored when you don't see the results you want right away.

Patience really is a virtue.

18. Intelligence: While many people think of intelligence as something to talk about in hushed tones, there's no denying that intelligent people are the people most likely to succeed.

19. Confidence: We've gone over this tons, but the point is that if you don't believe in you: no one else is going to either.

20. Originality: Originality in ideas, temperament and everything else is one of the most valuable traits there are. To be truly successful you can either be the best, or the first. Guess which is easier? True originals stand out, they're remembered and they have no competition.

Chapter 6

SPEAK AND GET WHAT YOU WANT CORRECTLY

Persuasion Basics

In a world where man does not stand alone or where getting something done often involves either the assistance of other people or the participation of them, it would be prudent to learn some skills that would make this a easy exercise.

One of the skills worth knowing and exercising is the art of persuasion. There are several tactics, formats or ideas that can be successfully applied to master the art of persuasion and here are just a few of them:

- Starting out with an understanding approach or attitude is perhaps one of the better ways of putting the other party at ease immediately. Being seen as relating to their predicament helps to build the platform of comfortable acceptance and openness. Reflecting some of the characteristics of the other party also helps to build trust as then the sense of really understanding is perceived.

- Providing an atmosphere that is both friendly and inviting is also another good way to increase the percentage of successful persuasion. Little things like making sincere compliments can sometimes be the extra ingredient that makes the persuasion technique more believable. People who feel worthy often are more willing to go the extra mile to please.

- Being able to provide compelling and substantiated evidence certainly elevates the chances of successfully persuading someone to do anything. Making sure of course that the evidence or claims is verifiable thus also ensuring a good and bankable reputation in the process.

- Providing practical guidelines and plausible solutions also helps the persuasive argument to gain support. When designing proposals that need persuasive arguments, ensure that all material linked to the argument are well prepared and error proof. Being well prepare is always an admirable quality and definitely a good persuasion tool. Confidence is also another quality that goes well when using the persuasion technique. A confident person is taken seriously and respected for his or her opinions.

Know How To Pick Your Battles

Often people instinctively feel the need to fight and win every battle, big or small daily. This is not only exhausting but can be so stressful that they inadvertently forget to enjoy life in general.

Every now and then, everyone should learn to make a conscious effort take a step back and examine the need to address every battle and understand that it is not always wise or necessary to get involved, and that walking away may just be a better solution. Learning to wisely discern which battle to fight is explored in the following points:

- Patience – often a virtue most people are unable to master. Though it has been popularly noted that older or more experienced individual are better able to exercise this virtue when it comes to the question of choosing the battles to fight. When patience is exercised, things may be worked out without actually having to participate in any "battle".

- Learning to be more accepting and letting go of rigid mindsets allows an individual the freedom of not having to be judgmental and easily provoked. Because of this more accommodative mindset, some battles are easier to overlook and thus reducing the constant need to control everything.

- Avoid getting involved in matters that either doesn't concern the individual or where the individual's knowledge is limited. Getting involved when ill equipped only brings about confusion and problems that eventually make an originally small matter become something that is blown out of proportion.

- Weight all possible repercussions and consequences before taking on any battle. Without doing this simple yet extremely important and beneficial exercise, the individual may find that the battle is all consuming and damaging both mentally and physically and may be even financially unsound.

- Questioning the intention and merits of getting involved in the battle is also advised before actually embarking on what may well be a useless waste of time and effort.

Know What You Want The Outcome To Be

It is always easier to embark on something when there is tangible goal in mind. Working towards this can not only be done in a systematic manner but can also have a higher level of success rate attached to it. This element of probable success is an element most sought after when venturing into any foray.

Having a fair idea of what is needed, what is desired and the eventual outcome is instrumental is several different areas that are normally addressed at the onset stages of an endeavor.

Issues such as manpower, expertise, equipment, time frames, budgets and many other related matters have to discuss and accessed once the desired outcome is clearly outlined. Tailoring all these elements to ensure the originally desired outcome is reached as adequately as possible is one of the most important items that most planning process takes into account.

Other aspects that are often considered when exploring the possible outcome scenarios is the ability to create allowances that can be applied should the need arise so as not to derail the expected outcome too much.

If an individual or group is unable to clearly identify the desired outcome for any plan, then working out the step by step process to achieve the said plan cannot be done properly, therefore the importance of knowing or having a specific outcome expectation in place is vital.

Also because the desired outcome is clearly outlined a check and balance format can also be drawn up and studied from time to time through the course of the endeavor. Adjustments and improvements can be easily made if the desired outcome is easily understood by all involved. With a clear picture in mind as to the outcome expected, it is also easier to work wise and effectively towards achieving the goal as opposed to simply working "blindly" without direction or knowledge of what the expected outcome is.

The motivation element present in the knowledge of a clearly outlined goal is also something not to be underestimated.

Empathize And Identify With Who you Are Speaking To

Being able to empathize and identify with people one is interacting with, usually provides the much needed edge to take the interaction to the next stage. Even being perceived as doing so has its advantages. Most relationships and interactions especially in the business world come with some level of reservations and guardedness. Therefore it is important to be able to shown the characteristic often and well.

There are several advantages to being able to empathize or identify with others and some of them are depicted below:

- By showing a little empathy towards others, the individual is able to gain the confidence and warmth that may be needed to enlist the help of others easily and effectively. When people are able to comfortably identify with others they are more likely to go along with suggestions and be more helpful in any given situation. Work becomes more productive and better in quality too.

- Using empathy usually requires some level of love and warmth and this trait is highly respected and always sought after. People are more willing to be associated with individuals who have this quality. Team leaders are especially successful when they are able to portray some levels of showing empathy as this gives the impression of being able to identify on some level with what the other person maybe going through.

- The working environment also becomes less threatening and hostile and instead more conducive when some levels of empathy are clearly present. Individuals are more likely to voice their concerns and at the other end of the spectrum are also able to relate better to the concerns being brought up, rather than simply disregarding everything that is deemed inconsequential or unrelated.

- Personal gains are put on hold for the betterment of others when an individual is able to experience empathy from being able to relate better to the unfortunate situation at hand.

Speak Confidently

Most successful people may not be very knowledgeable but when they speak they come across as so because of the confidence levels evident in the way they present themselves and in their speech. Speaking confidently definitely creates the platform for respect and attention which is very important when one is trying to make a point. Confidence is something that should be mastered is one expects to be taken seriously in any situation.

Being able to speak confidently does not necessarily mean being very knowledgeable in a particular subject though it does not hurt to be so. More importantly one needs to be able to show the said confidence in a convincing manner that gives an aura of authority that should be questioned.

When the art of speaking confidently is suitable achieved, the individual will be able to command the attention of almost anyone at anytime with little or no effort at all.

People who are able to speak confidently are often

admired and the information being presented is also often simply accepted without question. This is mostly due to the body posture and strength behind the vocal delivery which exudes confidence.

In order to be able to speak confidently an individual must have as much relevant information as possible. In some cases the need to "practice" before making the presentation is called for but as the confidence level builds up, this need decreases accordingly.

When the information being presented is both well researched and understood by the speaker, the delivery will naturally be done with some level of confidence. This is probably due to the fact that the speaker is more that capable of addressing any questions and concerns regarding the said information presented.

Being involved in as many situations as possible with the intention of practicing the portrayal of confidence also helps to further refine this skill. Participating in vocal exchanges regularly will also help to eventually contribute to the confidence levels of an individual.

The Importance Of Learning From Your Encounter

An essential part of self-improvement is learning from the various encounters one is exposed to on a daily basis. Several positive attributes can be derived from these encounters which can be successfully applied in future similar situations.

This is mainly because some idea of possible outcomes are already learnt, seen or experienced. Essentially the experience only becomes beneficial if something has been learnt from the encounter.

Below are just some of the elements that can be learnt and then applied in any future circumstances to ensure better outcomes.

- When one is able to learn to apologies and yet retain some semblance of dignity, previous encounters that could have benefitted from this reaction will now be looked upon as a good learning curve.

- Learning to adjust one's expectations based on previous encounters will allow the individual to better relate to other people with certain shortcomings. It will also enable to individual to control the urge to be a perfectionist and expect the same from those around.

- Understanding the whys and hows from past encounters also keeps the individual from making the same mistakes. However if the mistake is repeated than the individual is better equipped to deal with the situation and its consequences.

- Learning from past encounters is also a great way of turning an unpleasant experience into a workable and perhaps even beneficial opportunity. The wisdom gained from the encounter will give the individual the edge needed to take better calculated risks if the need arises.

Conclusion

A good quote is always welcome, especially if it digs into something real, something raw, and something true. Check out these 15 quotes on the subject and see if there are any that reach out and grab you:

"It is very important to understand that Emotional Intelligence, is not the opposite of Intelligence, it is not the triumph of heart over head. It is the unique intersection of both."

David Caruso

"Some people think only intellect counts: knowing how to solve problems, knowing how to get by, knowing how to identify an advantage and seize it. But the functions of intellect are insufficient without courage, love, friendship, compassion, and empathy."

Dean Koontz

"Unleash in the right time and place before you explode at the wrong time and place."

Oli Anderson

"Leadership is not domination, but the art of persuading people to work toward a common goal."

Daniel Goleman

"I've learned that people will forget what you said, people will forget what you did, but people will never forget how you made them feel."

Anonymous (but often attributed to Maya Angelou)

"The greatest ability in business is to get along with others and influence their actions."

John Hancock

"Emotional intelligence is a way of recognizing, understanding, and choosing how we think, feel, and act. It shapes our interactions with others and our

understanding of ourselves. It defines how and what we learn; it allows us to set priorities; it determines the majority of our daily actions. Research suggests it is responsible for as much as 80 percent of the "success" in our lives."

J. Freedman

"People who keep stiff upper lips find that it's damn hard to smile."

Judith Guest

"Our feelings are not there to be cast out or conquered. They're there to be engaged and expressed with imagination and intelligence."

T.K. Coleman

"In my 35 years in business, I have always trusted my emotions. I have always believed that by touching emotion you get the best people to work with you, the best clients to inspire you, the best partners and most devoted customers."

Kevin Roberts

"When dealing with people, remember you are not dealing with creatures of logic, but with creatures of emotion."

Dale Carnegie

"A leader is a dealer in hope."

Napoleon Bonaparte

"No one cares how much you know, until they know how much you care."

Theodore Roosevelt

"Emotions are not problems to be solved. They are signals to be interpreted."

Vironika Tugaleva

"As much as 80% of adult "success" comes from Emotional Intelligence."

Daniel Goleman

Be the Person You Want to Be

So there you have it! That's pretty much how you need to start changing the way you think if you want to be truly successful. It takes time, it takes work and it takes practice – but if you're able to put in the hours then you will find that the result is that you transform your brain into an incredibly powerful tool capable of helping you to get anything that you want. To recap, what have we learned?

We've learned that your thought patterns really do make a huge difference to your success. This is no coincidence. To be successful you need to believe in your success, you need to take risks and you need to be willing to keep trying.

We've learned that writing plans and strategies in the right way can help you to minimize your risk and to succeed beyond your wildest dreams. If you're willing to bet on yourself and to take massive action you can do incredible things – and we've seen plenty of amazing examples of that.

What's more, we've also learned how to change our thinking. It's all well and good to say you 'need to think this way' but without being able to make those permanent changes this is all just theory. Using cognitive behavioral therapy, cognitive restructuring, mindfulness, thought challenges, positive affirmations, fear setting, priming and more we've learned that the brain can be hacked and rewired to more closely emulate the brains of the world's most successful people.

We've also gone over briefly how human intelligence works and how you can nourish the brain to encourage learning, growth and intelligence.

Finally, we've looked at the traits that the world's most successful people share in common.

Now you have the tools and the blueprint to change your thinking and to get that 'limitless brain' you need to make anything happen. Just:

- Assess your goals
- Create a plan
- Restructure your thoughts
- Execute

It's as easy as that but without those vital first steps where you change the way you think, you stand very little chance of success.

And don't forget to improve your social skills and increase your emotional intelligence!

- Work on Your Communication Skills
- Improve Your Conflict Management Skills
- Improve Your Leadership Skills
- Develop Persuasion and Influencing Skills
- Work on Building Rapport

When you have high emotional intelligence, it's obvious based on your social skills. If you want to improve your emotional intelligence, then you need to work on these five ways for developing both your social skills and leadership.